The Private Life of the Otter

Philip Wayre

B.T. Batsford Ltd *London*

First published 1979
© Philip Wayre 1979

ISBN 0 7134 0833 2

Filmset in 'Monophoto' Photina by
Servis Filmsetting Ltd, Manchester

Printed in Great Britain
by The Anchor Press Ltd, Tiptree, Essex
for the publishers B.T. Batsford Ltd
4 Fitzhardinge Street, London W1H 0AH

The Private Life of the Otter

Contents

Acknowledgments

I wish to record my grateful thanks to all those field workers and scientists who have given me the benefit of their advice, personal observations and opinions.

Together with my publishers, I am grateful to the following for their permission to reproduce material. To Blandford Press for the line drawings on pages 17, 88 and 91, which were taken from *Mammals of Britain: Their Tracks, Trails and Signs* by M.J. Lawrence and R.W. Brown (second edition 1974); to Jean Webb and the Mammal Society for the line drawing on page 38; to Radio Times Hulton Picture Library for the photograph on page 64 and Popperfoto for the photograph on page 66.

To Ripple, Kate and Lucy

Introduction

'On watching a gambolling fox cub, a fawn, an ocelot, a marten, or even a well-furred pet skunk, one is apt to be carried away and declare each in turn the most beautiful and graceful creature ever seen. But when all are gone from view, when nothing but the dim impression remains it is the otter that stands out pre-eminently as the most beautiful and engaging of all pets.'

So wrote that famous and most competent naturalist, Ernest Seton, back in 1926 and nobody who has ever kept a tame otter cub would disagree with him.

Perhaps the best way to gain an idea of an otter's life is to follow an imaginary animal as it sets out on its nightly wandering on a lowland river in East Anglia.

In early summer the marshes are full of bird song, reed warblers keep up their motonous cadence from the swaying stems and sedge warblers utter their rasping notes as they creep mouse-like through the tangle of riverside vegetation. The hemlock is already a metre high and will double its growth before the days begin to shorten.

The first lapwings have already hatched, tiny balls of grey and black fluff moving across the marsh like clockwork toys on unsteady legs, while overhead their parents wail hysterically at every intruder. As the sun sinks behind the trees, throwing long shadows across the meadows, the birds fall silent and soon the plop of a fish snatching an early sedge fly and the clicking of a hawking bat are the only sounds. The lowing of a distant cow carries far on the evening air. . . .

The otter, a dog in his fourth year, had spent the hours of daylight asleep beneath the wooden floor of the old boathouse. It was one of his favourite places, near the centre of his territory. The boathouse had not been used for more than a decade and already the roof had begun to sag, ivy had smothered one gable and the concrete slipway, empty of boats, was moss-grown. The whole place was gloomy and dank, but the earth beneath the floor boards of the store-room was warm and dry.

A short distance away the river flowed deep and dark and since the land was private and overgrown with nettles and goose-grass no one disturbed the peace. The otter slept curled up, his chin resting on his rudder and it was almost dark before he moved. Then he woke and yawned before stretching full length, his belly on the ground, forepaws fully extended and his hind legs thrust out behind him. He yawned again, then gathered himself and crawled out onto the edge of the slipway. There he paused and looked around, his whiskers twitching and his small ears pricked, listening. Satisfied, he dropped down onto the concrete ramp, wandered to the far side and sniffed carefully at a moss-covered brick dislodged from the side wall. Then he turned round, back arched, and with his rudder lifted, he deposited some spraint on the flat top of

8

the brick. Again he yawned, then slid into the water and slipped beneath the surface leaving scarcely a ripple behind him. Only the white barn owl, who had a nest in the roof, saw him go.

A European otter at the edge of a weir.

To human eyes the water was dark and forbidding, visibility scarcely an arm's length, but the otter could see clearly and his whiskers reinforced his vision. To him the underwater world was as familiar as his regular route through the reed beds and across the marshes. He recognized every bed of swaying weed, knew the pathways between them and where to find the shoals of roach and chub that glided across the bed of the river like grey torpedoes.

He travelled upstream keeping to the centre of the river and surfacing only to take breath. Beyond the first bend lay the old road bridge that had once carried the main road. An ancient wooden signpost, half obscured by a straggling hawthorn hedge, still told the traveller that northbound the way led to

9

Yarmouth and south to London, more than 100 miles away. The lettering was small by modern standards and the height just right for a man on horseback. The old bridge was scarcely wide enough to take a stage coach and beneath its vaulted stone arches the river ran deep and clear.

In more recent times the ancient buttresses had been reinforced with concrete, leaving a sill 30 centimetres wide well above the water level. Beneath the right hand arch the dog otter stopped and jumped on to the sill. At the far end he paused and sniffed at some shining black spraint no bigger than a beetle. It was moist and fresh and the smell told him that a bitch otter had passed that way earlier in the evening. Turning round he raised his rudder and added his contribution, for this was a regular sprainting place and one that he rarely failed to visit on his journeyings up and down the river.

Beyond the new bridge with its sheer concrete pillars the river became shallow, babbling over a bed of pebbles black with algae. Here and there patches of water celery managed to find a root-hold between the stones, forming a mat of bright green leaves.

This was the place to find crayfish, small grey-brown freshwater lobsters rarely more than eight centimetres long. They spent the day hiding beneath the stones or in holes in the bank and at night emerged to hunt for dragonfly larvae, water snails and other small aquatic creatures upon which they fed. The otter plodded through the shallows, the water rippling over his head as he nosed under the stones. Suddenly a crayfish darted away, flipping itself backwards with jerky movements of its tail. The otter pounced and caught it easily then he lay in the shallows holding it in his forepaws while he ate noisily, crunching the hard pincer claws.

Further upstream the floor of the valley widened and the river had carved a serpentine course through the flat expanse of grazing marshes, intersected by straight drainage dykes fringed with reed-grass and sedge. Coypu were common and the waterside vegetation had been cut back by their continual nibbling. Originally imported from South America to be farmed for their fur, some had escaped and become naturalized in the East Anglian waterways where they flourished, despite efforts to stamp them out by organized trapping.

The otter left the river to hunt the dykes for eels and moorhens. He soon caught a smallish eel, nosing it out of the black mud, and swam with it to the bank where he ate it, lying half awash among the rushes. He caught two more eels in the next hour, then made his way back to the river, stopping to spraint where a barbed wire fence crossed the dyke. The grass near one of the fence posts had grown green from years of otter spraint, for this was another regular site.

Where the river doubled back on itself the otter left the water and took a short cut, loping across the open marsh. It was a traditional route ending in a short slide down the steep bank where it rejoined the river. When travelling on land devoid of cover the otter increased his pace, nervous of being caught out in the open.

Midnight found him more than five kilometres upstream of the old boathouse and shortly afterwards, he passed silently beneath Shotford bridge, past the cottage gardens where the river skirted the village. A light glowed orange in an upstairs window and he heard voices, then a car started up and

10

moved off down the main road.

Not far from the village a hollow ash tree, victim of lightning at the height of a summer storm 20 years before, lay sprawled out into the meadow, its roots just clear of the water. The otter climbed up the bank and rolled in the grass to dry his coat, squirming from side to side and rubbing his chin backwards and forwards on the ground. Then he rolled over onto his back and wriggled this way and that until his coat was completely dry. Crawling inside the tree trunk he scratched a hollow in the rotten wood, curled up and was soon asleep.

Summer nights are short and only four hours later a pale green light spread slowly across the eastern sky. The otter woke and shook himself as he left the hollow tree; stretching and yawning he moved slowly along the top of the bank and dropped down onto a grass-covered ledge where he left his spraint before slipping into the water. Soon he caught a roach, about 15 centimetres long, and ate it on the bank, devouring the whole fish in less than five minutes.

In the quiet reaches below Hoxne he found the bitch otter with whom he had mated the previous year. Her two cubs had remained with her for ten months and had only recently become independent, the male cub wandering off on his own while the female remained in the vicinity.

The two otters greeted each other with low whickering notes as they touched noses, then the female dived and swam away. The dog otter gave chase and the two animals corkscrewed through the water, twisting and turning, diving and spinning. Once the dog made a half-hearted attempt to mate with the bitch, but she was not ready and tore herself free. They swam together for some time but parted company when the dog otter left the river to follow the mill leat where the deep water scarcely moved. He swam right up to the sluice gate at the head of the channel before turning back, hunting the deeps for eels.

At sun-up a curtain of white mist rose like steam from the marshes and soon the larks began to climb above it singing, lapwings wailed and tumbled in acrobatic flight and a cuckoo called from the poplar plantation beyond the white farmhouse. Hours of patient watching from the tops of willow and alder trees had taught her the whereabouts of every reed warbler's nest in her territory and its state of readiness. One, not far away from the poplar plantation, had been completed two days earlier and the hen reed warbler was about to lay her first egg in it. The female cuckoo was conditioned to lay on the same day and so she watched and waited. As soon as the reed warbler had laid her egg the cuckoo would glide down into the reed bed, remove the reed warbler's egg in her bill and deposit her own in its place.

Unsuspecting, the hen reed warbler would complete her clutch only to have all her eggs thrown out by the young cuckoo within hours of its hatching.

The dog otter made his way to the alder carr above Hoxne bridge and there he left the water and rolled himself dry on the bank. The ground was marshy and covered by a dense thicket of nettles, bramble and goose-grass. The otter crept into the thickest part and hollowed out a bed beneath the brambles. There he curled up and slept away the hours of daylight. He was awakened around noon by a farm tractor passing along the edge of the spinney, but the sound soon died away and he slept again, only twitching his whiskers at a bluebottle, which buzzed lazily round his head. . . .

1 – The otter

Otters are found in all parts of the world except in Australia and New Zealand, Madagascar and the Arctic and Antarctic regions. According to Harris (1968) there are 19 accepted species and very many more sub-species or races. However, many of these sub-species or races appear to have been based on too little scientific evidence and too few specimens to be valid.

Belonging to a group of animals known as Mustelids or Mustelidae, otters are related to stoats, weasels, polecats, mink, martens and even to wolverines, skunks and badgers. As would be expected in animals with such a world-wide distribution the different species of otter show a considerable diversity in size and other characteristics ranging from the smallest, the Asian Short-clawed Otter *Amblonyx cinerea*, around 75 cm (30 in.) in length to the giant Brazilian *Pteronura brasiliensis* which may grow to almost 2.75 cm (9 ft) in length.

European otter cubs 14 weeks old.

A Eurasian otter, *Lutra l. barang*, standing up to greet visitors at the Norfolk Wildlife Park, Great Witchingham.

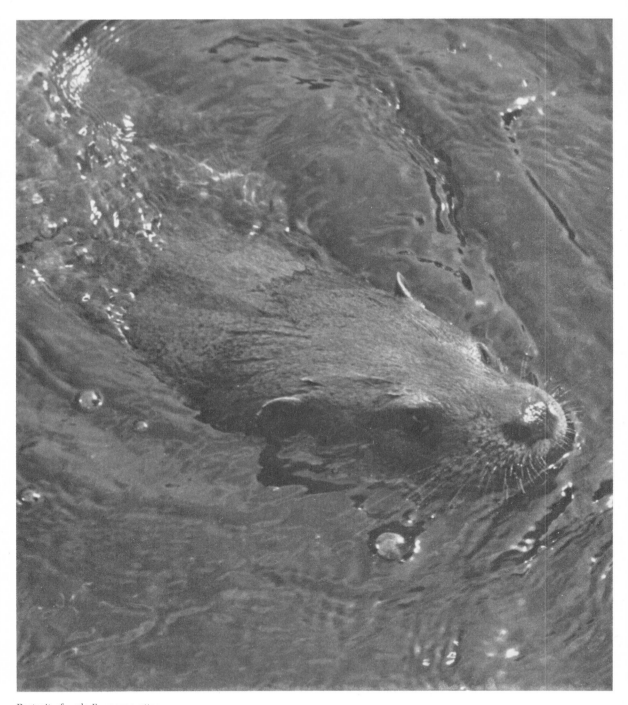

Portrait of male European otter
showing characteristic W
shape to the rhinarium or
muzzle.

As soon as an otter leaves the
water its coat breaks into an
irregular spiky pattern caused
by the outer guardhairs
sticking together.

15

This book is concerned with the European otter which is found in the United Kingdom and Ireland and throughout Europe, south to Morocco and Algeria, and in Asia, as far north approximately as the Arctic Circle, south to the Himalayas and eastward into Taiwan and Japan. In Asia various races are recognized, several of them occurring in the region of the Himalayas and beyond.

Of these Asian races the only one of which I have experience and have bred regularly is *Lutra lutra barang* from south-eastern Asia. It is like its European cousin, but considerably smaller and much paler beneath the neck and chin.

The otter possesses the usual family characteristics of the Mustelidae, including two scent glands below the base of the rudder or tail. Being semi-aquatic it is specially adapted for life in water while still able to live and move fast on land.

The otter is a thickset animal with a long body and short, loosely articulated legs. Its neck is compact and as thick as its broad, almost snakelike head. The body is muscular and streamlined, reaching its maximum width at the hips and ending in a long and powerful tail. This is fully covered by hair and tapers from a broad base to a slender tip. Somewhat flattened horizontally it is used in swimming as a means of propulsion and is also used to help the otter to turn quickly underwater, as well as acting as a brace or third leg when the animal stands up on its hind legs to obtain a better view on land.

The two small scent glands at the base of the rudder contain a strong-smelling milky-white substance which is used sparingly to mark the otter's territory. However, if an otter is badly frightened, it will release a quantity of this fluid, especially if struggling to escape capture.

Underwater an otter can attain a speed of 11 km/h (7 mph) (Harris 1968), or even more in short bursts. It propels itself by flexing its rear quarters and rudder (dorso-ventral flexion) in powerful vertical strokes like the tail flukes of a whale, but on the surface it dog-paddles with all four feet, a much slower means of progression.

The eyes of otters are upturned and small and on land their sight is rather poor, but beneath the water their vision is remarkably good. The ears are small and like the valvular nostrils can be closed at will when the animal is submerged.

Despite having lungs of large air capacity, the left with two lobes and the right with four, otters cannot remain underwater for more than three to four minutes at the most and usually dives are of far shorter duration. They occasionally descend to considerable depths and there is a record of a North American otter being drowned in a crab-pot which was set in water 18 metres (60 ft) deep (Scheffer 1953).

Otters are impervious to conditions that are close to freezing owing to their thick, water-repellent coat. This consists of an underlayer of very dense waterproof fur protected by an outer covering of longer and stiffer guard hairs. When the animal dives air is trapped between the two layers providing further insulation. The pressure of water forces the air out in the characteristic chain of bubbles. When diving with my tame otters I have noticed that bubbles of air also leave the corners of the mouth and, curling upwards, unite with those from the fur, so that a continual stream is forced back along the otter's body.

16

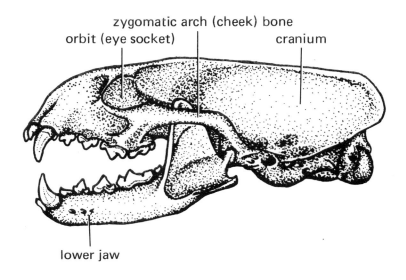

zygomatic arch (cheek) bone

orbit (eye socket)   cranium

lower jaw

ABOVE A lateral view of the
skull of a European otter.

BELOW Ventral view.

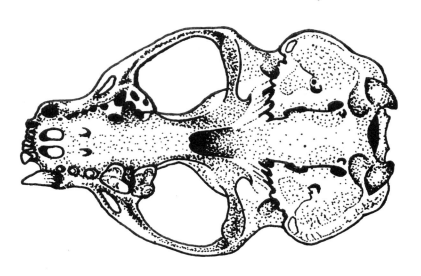

Such fine fur has to be kept in immaculate condition if it is to remain waterproof and otters spend a great deal of their time on land rolling and rubbing themselves dry and grooming their coats. This they do with a clipper-like, nibbling motion of their incisor-teeth. As soon as an otter leaves the water its coat breaks into an irregular spiky pattern caused by the outer guard hairs sticking together. An otter forced to remain too long in the water gradually becomes sodden, waterlogged and cold. This can result in death by exposure.

Anyone who has studied otters can easily recognize the footprints or 'seals' made by the five widely separated toes on each foot. All five toes may not show up clearly, but the rounded appearance of the print and the ball under the sole of the foot, together with the flattening of the ridges between the toes caused by the inter-digital webs, are diagnostic.

The external senses of otters are well developed and that of sight has already been mentioned as better underwater than above. The sense of smell may be reasonably good, but is used less than the other senses. It is the otter's hearing which is used and relied upon most and it is remarkably acute. I have frequently observed my tame otters picking up and reacting to a sound, which was totally inaudible to human ears, as if they were receiving it on a different wavelength.

Next to hearing, the otter's whiskers or vibrissae may well provide the most important sense, certainly when the otter is hunting. The long, stiff whiskers are tactile and highly sensitive, being set in large nerve pads on each side of the snout, with two more clumps set further back below the chin on each side. In addition there are one or two whiskers on the face between the eye and the ear and on the 'elbow' of each foreleg.

Thanks to the work of Jim Green (1977) who carried out a series of experiments we now know just how sensitive and how important these vibrissae are. Briefly, Green discovered that it took an otter roughly four times as long to catch a fish in very cloudy water, 10 cm (4 in.) visibility to human eyesight, as it did in clear water.

Having ascertained this, Green removed all the whiskers on one otter by clipping them. Tested again the otter averaged the same time to catch a fish in clear water thus showing that sight is the dominant sense under conditions where there is light. However, when the water was stained and visibility reduced to 10 cm (4 in.) again, the otter, minus its whiskers, took more than six times as long to catch a fish and often gave up without doing so. Had the pool used for the experiment been larger it seems likely that the otter would have been less successful. It should also be remembered that cutting off the whiskers, which incidentally grow again quite quickly, does not destroy the tactile sense completely, but only reduces its efficiency since the nerve endings which connect with the vibrissae are still present.

The otter's skull is short, broad and flattened with a well developed occipital region. The skull itself is thin and therefore vulnerable to blows. The jaw is short and powerful with an interlocking hinge and teeth which are adapted to crushing bones. As the otter's gullet is small the animal chews its food thoroughly and does not bolt it like a dog. In captivity otters, especially old animals, seem prone to infections of the teeth and this may also occur in the wild.

Dog otters have an *os penis*, a bone once coveted by otter hunters which they made into tie pins. It varies in size and the largest measured by Marie Stephens (1957) was more than 6 cm ($2\frac{1}{2}$ in.) long and 1 cm ($\frac{3}{8}$ in.) in diameter. That this bone is often damaged or broken is confirmed by Stephens who examined a number of dead otters. It is commonly believed that the damage is done when rival males fight, but there is a lack of reliable evidence to support this.

Individual otters vary in size, dogs being a good deal larger and heavier than bitches. A dog otter can measure up to 120 cm (48 in.) or even more in length and can weigh up to 14 kg (30 lb), although the average is probably nearer 11 kg (24 lb). A bitch may reach 12.3 kg (28 lb) with 7.4 kg (16 lb) a fair average.

It is usually quite easy to distinguish a dog from a bitch otter, if the animal can be seen closely and full face. The dog's muzzle is broader and deeper and the general appearance of the head wider between the ears.

2 – Territory and behaviour

The otter, a wanderer by nature, needs a large territory and on a lowland river of average size, say 15–20 m (16–22 yds) wide a dog may require as much as 20 km (12½ miles) for its home range. A bitch otter requires less space, up to 11 km (7 miles) of river and so it is possible for more than one bitch to have her territory within the range of a single dog otter. Most of the work upon which these measurements are based was carried out in Sweden (Erlinge, 1969). However it seems likely that the otter's range may be as large or even larger in some areas of lowland Britain.

These are only rough guidelines and there is still much to be learned about the habits of otters in the wild. However it seems certain that the size of territory varies considerably according to the type of habitat and available food supply. An otter may need a much smaller territory under ideal conditions, including maximum cover and food, and minimum disturbance. But where conditions are not so suitable it may be forced to range even further.

Bitch otters with young cubs are very aggressive so it seems unlikely that the territories of two bitches would normally overlap. But Bobby Tulloch (1976), warden for the Royal Society for the Protection of Birds in Shetland, who has studied otters there, has observed two different and recognizable bitch otters using the same holt, although at different times.

I do not believe that otters are particularly aggressive towards each other except when the bitch has cubs or the dog is intent on mating. On the few occasions when we have inadvertently put two animals of the same sex in one enclosure there has never been any serious fighting and usually they have settled down amicably together.

Otters are found in a wide variety of habitats including slow-flowing coarse fish rivers, faster salmon and trout waters, lakes, tarns, marshes, both fresh and salt, and in some areas along the seashore.

During the day-time otters lie up in holts which are often burrows in the bank usually having one entrance underwater and at least one entrance well above high water mark. Sometimes the holts or burrows are located beneath the roots of fallen trees or among boulders by the riverside. The length varies from two to several metres, depending upon the soil conditions. The actual chamber is usually circular in shape and about 50 cm in diameter. In some parts of the country where there are dense reed beds, otters may make couches or platforms of reed and sometimes their cubs are born there. They are also particularly fond of lying up beneath dense stands of bramble, where they feel safe from marauders, and cubs are not infrequently born in such locations.

Unpolluted lowland rivers are usually rich in coarse fish and other vertebrate life. These waters, known to scientists as eutrophic, are the otter's first choice because of the abundant and easily caught food supply compared

OPPOSITE:
Entrance to an otter's holt beneath rocks on the shore of a Scottish sea loch.

with the comparatively barren or oligotrophic stretches of fast flowing trout rivers with their boulder-strewn courses and scarcity of aquatic life.

Unfortunately for the otter, lowland rivers are subject to tremendous pressures in a small, highly industrialized country like Britain. The marshes are drained and ploughed up for arable crops, the banks are cleared of vegetation, herbicides are sometimes used in dykes and ditches to kill aquatic plants upon which the life of the river depends, and all the time disturbance increases. More people have more leisure – there are more anglers, more pleasure boats, more canoes, more ramblers and bird watchers. In the face of such competition and loss of habitat it is small wonder that the otter, once abundant in lowland Britain, is now considered a rare animal even in its former strongholds.

It is perhaps significant that a healthy otter population still flourishes along the west coast of Scotland where deserted sea lochs with their rocky shores backed by wild moors and forest provide ideal habitat. Fish and crabs abound in the sea and the plentiful food may be the reason these coastal otters appear to have smaller territories than their inland cousins. In such undisturbed areas they are frequently diurnal and most active on an incoming tide when fish are more easily caught. The shoreline is often rocky with moorland coming down to the sea interspersed by sheltered spinneys of deciduous trees. Small sandy bays and plantations of conifers also occur and there are usually numerous spate streams coming down from the high moors.

Under these conditions the otters spend most of their lives on the coast though they sometimes leave the shore and follow the stream up into the hill lochs to hunt for trout, especially at spawning times. Their holts are often in

Entrances to an otter's holt beneath rocks on the shore of a Scottish sea loch.

OPPOSITE:
An otter's holt among rocks 30 metres from the shore of a Scottish sea loch.

23

An otter's couch or resting
place in a reed bed.

An otter's couch or lying-up
place at the edge of a Scottish
sea loch.

Otter habitat on the west coast of Scotland. Cubs were born on a couch in the centre of the clump of Yellow Flag *Iris pseudacorus*.

woodland only a few metres back from the high water mark. Sometimes these are excavated beneath the roots of trees, but are frequently underneath large rocks with two or more entrances. Such holts are fairly easy to find and if in regular use there is usually a well defined track leading up from the sea.

Holts on lowland rivers are much more difficult to locate and are sometimes well back from the main river up a side stream or drainage dyke. The entrance may be hidden beneath the roots of a tree growing on the bank or virtually underwater and screened by vegetation. In marshy areas the otter often makes use of hollow trees, drainage culverts or even couches or hovers consisting of a

bed of flattened reed or sedge well hidden in a thicket or reedbed. Otters are good climbers and will sometimes use the top of a pollard willow as a place in which to lie up.

Drying off places are also easier to locate along the shore since the ground has usually been rubbed bare, whereas on a lowland river the otter tends to dry itself on the grass or bank wherever it happens to come ashore.

Much has been written about the use otters make of slides and it is sometimes inferred that they make them deliberately. I do not believe this to be the case. I have seen slides along the shore, on islands in Scottish sea-lochs and

Drying-off place overlooking a Scottish sea loch. If disturbed the otter could dive straight into the water several metres below.

27

on lowland rivers, but they are not things one finds frequently and those I have examined have been made quite by chance; in most cases because the otter's traditional path has traversed a steep bank or slope and the surface has become worn and slippery with use. The otter quickly discovers that it is easier to toboggan down the slope especially if it is wet, and so a slide is made.

This does not mean that otters never consciously use a slide in play. I am sure they do and I recall finding quite a long slide down a steep and very wet peat bank more than a metre high on an island in a sea loch. A trickle of water ran from a marshy area up on the hillside, down the slide and into a small pool filled with sedge and rushes. In the middle of the pool there was a large rock on a mound and abundant evidence that the otters had been running round and round the rock, up the bank where the slope was shallow and back down the slide into the pool. The tracks were worn smooth and when I found the place they were still wet with recent use.

It is well known that otters are playful creatures and I have frequently seen adults playing together especially when two otters are reunited after a spell apart. Single otters will play with anything that catches their attention – a shell, a feather, a round pebble, almost any small object – but they soon become bored and start looking for something new.

A fresh fall of snow offers otters endless opportunity for play and there is nothing they like more than to rush along, nose beneath the surface, furrowing the snow like a snow plough and leaving the impression of one long slide. If the surface is strong enough to bear its weight the otter may run for a few steps, then slide along on its stomach with its forelegs tucked back by its side. Such slides may be more than three metres long if conditions are right.

Otters are little affected by harsh weather as long as they can keep open a hole in the ice through which they can continue to fish, returning to the hole periodically for air.

The otters' use of traditional routes or pathways sometimes leads to their undoing especially when they happen to cross a main road. I know of two places in Norfolk where, in the last 20 years, several otters have been run over by cars at exactly the same spot. In both places known to me it is clear that the road has bisected an otter's territory, leaving important feeding areas on both sides of it. Such pathways are usually what might be termed 'main' routes, which may well have been used by otters long before the roads were built.

Otters sometimes travel far from water especially when moving from one river system to another. At such times they will lie up in any convenient place including rabbit burrows.

An otter marks its territory in a number of ways, the most important being by depositing its faeces, called spraint, in traditional places. These sprainting sites may occur on ledges or sills beneath bridges, on small promontories at the confluence of a river and a side stream, on sandspits, or on large boulders, or even fallen tree trunks.

The nightly behaviour of an otter varies considerably in different types of habitat. For example it is often very difficult to find regular sprainting places on a lowland river unless the bridges have suitable sills or sand bars beneath them, whereas on a trout stream in Wales or the West Country large boulders are regularly chosen and these sprainting sites are fairly easy to monitor.

OPPOSITE:
An otter's slide down a peat bank more than one metre high.

29

Pathway made by otters playing round and round a large rock in the centre of a peat bog. The slide was situated near by.

30

An otter's pathway leading to a drying-off place at the edge of a Scottish sea loch.

3 – Food and feeding habits

Otters are carnivores and fish may account for 70 per cent or more of their diet; the remainder being made up of crayfish, frogs, birds and mammals.

By examining stomach contents and analyzing the remains of prey in samples of spraint (see page 38), scientists have established the wide range of animal life upon which the otter lives. As would be expected, its diet varies according to the habitat and the availability of prey species.

The Swedish scientist, Dr S. Erlinge, has shown (1969) that where coarse fish, such as turbot, roach, chub, bream, pike and perch occur in the same water as trout, the former comprise more than 90 per cent of the otter's diet and trout less than 10 per cent.

This appears to be confirmed by Stephens (1957) who reported that a large collection of spraint from Lyneham Reservoir in Wiltshire consisted solely of numerous stickleback bones. The reservoir was well stocked with rainbow trout and sticklebacks were the only other fish present. Other workers have also confirmed the otter's preference for coarse fish in rivers where trout also occur. Weir and Bannister (1977) examined spraints from the River Glaven in Norfolk in 1972, a year when trout were common in the river having escaped from a trout farm upstream. No trout remains were found in the spraints. Of 47 collections of spraint from their study area, 46 contained the remains of sticklebacks, 42 eel, 10 cyprinid (roach and chub) and 13 cottid (bullheads, miller's thumb). Remains of other fish, crayfish, crabs, birds, mammals and frogs or toads were found in a much smaller proportion of collections.

I have studied my tame otters swimming completely free in the rivers of East Anglia. Wearing wet suit and aqualung, I have followed them underwater and have seen them pursue and take fish on many occasions and I am quite certain that they always go for the species that are easiest to catch. Eels are without doubt the otter's favourite and next come members of the carp family (cyprinids), the roach, rudd, bream, chub and dace. Perch and pike, especially small specimens, are also taken but fast-swimming species like trout and those that skulk in dense weed beds, like tench, are rarely taken.

Although otters will eat fish as small as sticklebacks and on occasion quite large pike or salmon, they catch mainly medium-sized specimens around 15 centimetres in length and I suspect this is because these are the easiest to take as well as being more abundant than larger fish.

In some rivers crayfish are frequently taken by otters. Their flesh is sweet by human standards and as they are small the otter sometimes devours the whole animal, crunching up the hard carapace and pincer claws.

An otter will eat any small bird it can catch. Wild duck are often taken but the moorhen appears to be the otter's favourite bird and one of the easiest for it to catch. I have seen my tame otters take them by an underwater attack,

OPPOSITE:
Fish scales from a large cyprinid eaten by an otter.

pulling the moorhen under by a leg or pouncing on them in thick vegetation.

One day last summer a pair of my European otters caught and killed an adult carrion crow in their enclosure and carried it into their den, though they made no attempt to eat it. I have also known them catch black-headed gulls though again, without eating them.

I have seen several mallard which have been killed by wild otters and on one occasion I arrived on the scene only minutes after the attack and saw the duck lying dead on a spit of land jutting out into Hoveton broad in Norfolk. The promontory was heavily overgrown with alder trees and it took me some time to find a place to land from the rowing boat. When I did the mallard had disappeared and all I found was a solitary otter print in the soft mud at the edge of the water.

In my experience an otter usually eats only the breast of a duck, picking it clean. While it may do the same to a moorhen, it quite often devours much more of it.

Frogs are another favourite food item and the otter enjoys catching them rather as a cat plays with a mouse. I have watched the chase many times and always feel sorry for the frog. The otter keeps pushing with its nose until the wretched frog leaps, only to be prodded into activity again until the otter, tiring of the game, decides to eat it, holding the frog in its forepaws while chewing. Contrary to popular belief the otter eats the entire frog and does not leave the skin turned neatly inside out as some writers have claimed. That is the work of rats, which also deal with toads in the same manner.

Small mammals, especially rabbit, also form part of the otter's diet and the following have been identified in spraints (Stephens, 1957): mole, shrew, hare (probably a leveret), bank vole, water vole and field vole. In some parts of Europe otters regularly prey on the introduced musk rats *Ondatra zibethicus,* especially during the winter.

Small quantities of vegetable matter have been found in otter spraint, but I think this was either eaten accidentally, perhaps when an otter was tearing up grass and sedge with its mouth to line its holt, or it was present in the stomach of the otter's prey.

Otters have also been reported feeding on carrion and Muller (1945) has suggested that bitch otters with young cubs are largely dependent on carrion. His observations were carried out in Yorkshire, but I can find no evidence to back them up although one or two keepers on the west coast of Scotland have told me that they are sure otters will eat sheep or lamb carrion when other food is scarce. Knowing from first hand observation underwater just how easy it is for an otter to catch fish I cannot believe that a bitch suckling cubs would waste time scouring the countryside for dead animals! If food were to be so scarce in the river it seems highly unlikely that the otter would stay there to breed.

If, as some people maintain, otters will eat carrion, this habit may be responsible for the accusations made, from time to time, that otters kill lambs or even sheep. As far as I know nobody has ever produced any real evidence that they do and I would wager that the killing has always been done by a fox or, even more probably, by stray dogs.

If otters regularly took carrion it would be a much simpler matter than it is to

study an individual animal's movements and hence its range, since it would be easy to include substances such as a dye or small coloured plastic beads in some carrion which would subsequently show up in the sprint. As far as I know this has never been accomplished.

Various writers have claimed that otters eat freshwater mussels *Anodonta cygnea*, but this has not been so in my experience. I have given captive otters both freshwater and salt water mussels *Mytilus edulis* on several occasions and they have never made any attempt to open the shells. Stephens (1957) fed freshwater mussels to her otters with the same results. However if the shells are broken open the otters will eat the contents readily.

Recently we put this theory to the test once again by giving 16 Eurasian otters, ten of them *Lutra l. lutra* and six *Lutra l. barang*, five freshly collected edible mussels each, on two consecutive evenings. Although the otters played with the mussels not one shell was opened or even cracked. Each morning the mussels were collected and replaced by fresh ones in the evening.

On the third day the 16 otters were again fed five mussels each, but this time all the mussels were fully opened before being given. All but three of the otters, one *Lutra l. lutra* and two *Lutra l. barang* ate the contents of all their mussel shells. Several otters were seen to do this holding the mussel down between the forepaws while nibbling at the contents with the front teeth and licking the shells clean.

Moss-covered stump on the River Waveney in Norfolk upon which a wild otter had eaten a large fish.

35

On each of the following four evenings, five fresh unopened mussels were again fed to all 16 otters, but none made any attempt whatever to crack them open. The mussels were either ignored or played with, then left unscathed. Since the otters made no attempt to crack open closed mussel shells, it seems possible that in the wild they only eat molluscs when they happen to find one with the shell already opened.

The otherwise vegetarian coypu is very fond of swan mussels, as are brown rats; both rodents will dive in search of the molluscs taking them onto the bank where they gnaw open the shells. Rats will dive to the bottom in 50 cm or more of water and coypu much deeper. Around the Norfolk Broads it is common to find large numbers of empty freshwater mussel shells at specific feeding places on the bank where the rodents regularly eat them.

An otter's teeth are designed for crushing bones and it eats a large object either by holding it down with its forepaws and tearing away mouthfuls of flesh, or, if the prey is not too big, by holding it in its front paws and chewing it with its molars, eating with the side of the mouth. This means that a large freshwater mussel would have to be splintered by the crushing action of the molars, whereas all the hundreds of empty shells I have examined have carried the unmistakable marks of gnawing by a rodent's incisor teeth.

The experiment described above does not of course prove that the otter never eats molluscs and Jan Veen (1975) claims that in north Holland freshwater mussels are regularly eaten by otters. Bearing in mind the great variety of prey taken by otters it is possible that some individuals have learned to eat molluscs. However, if this is so it seems probable that small fragments of shell would be discovered in the otter's spraint and so far as I know this has yet to be shown.

Otters living along the sea-shore take a wide variety of fish and on the west coast of Scotland, Jane Parker (1977) has observed them eating butterfish, saithe, flounders, lampfish, lobsters and even a cormorant. In the estuaries of Norfolk shore crabs, flounders and in brackish water sticklebacks have been recorded.

It is commonly held that otters will sometimes kill many more fish than they need simply for the fun of killing and while it is impossible to get hard evidence, there are so many accounts that some seem likely to be true. However, I have no first hand experience upon which to draw and no instance of such killing has ever been reported to me.

My otters have had many opportunities of indulging in a surfeit of killing for the fun of it, but I have never seen them kill more than one or two fish, usually eels, which they did not eat immediately. On the other hand I have seen them catch a fish for fun only to release it unharmed, but they quickly become bored with chasing fish unless they are hungry.

The weight of food eaten daily by an otter varies with the temperature of the air, the size of the otter and the type of food. Two of my adult European otters, both males weighing 12.25 kg and 10.9 kg respectively, were fed their usual meat-mix and fresh whiting ad lib for a week. Both were used to eating this food and liked it. Their enclosures were rat-proof and any food remaining uneaten was collected and weighed every morning and the results deducted from the weight given. The larger animal consumed on average 1.5 kg per day and the smaller 1.4 kg per day. Captive otters consume more food in cold

OPPOSITE:

Close-up of the remains of a large cyprinid eaten by an otter, showing scales and pharangeal teeth.

37

A

B

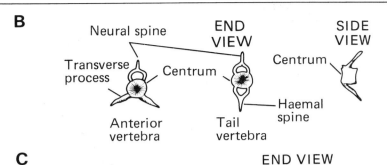

Neural spine — Transverse process — **END VIEW** — Centrum — **SIDE VIEW** — Centrum — Anterior vertebra — Tail vertebra — Haemal spine

C

END VIEW

Shiny vertebra with three spines when seen end on. 3–4 mm across. — STICKLEBACK

Spines opposite each other with wide bases. Vertebrae to 1 mm across. — STICKLEBACK

Spines arise opposite each other, bases equal. — CYPRINIDAE

Bone distinctly hook shaped, up to eight blunt teeth. — CYPRINIDAE (pharyngeal teeth)

A few examples of spraint analysis from Jean Webb's *Otter Spraint Analysis*. **A** shows actual remains. **B** The two kinds of vertebrae in a fish. Those from the anterior part of the body have processes sticking out sideways, but those from the tail region have the processes joined into one ventral haemal spine. **C** Several types of vertebrae and toothed bones often found in spraint analysis. **D** The otter's favourite food – eel.

D

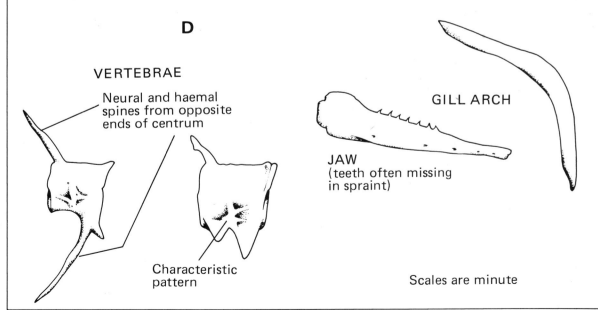

VERTEBRAE

Neural and haemal spines from opposite ends of centrum

Characteristic pattern

GILL ARCH

JAW (teeth often missing in spraint)

Scales are minute

38

weather and these tests were carried out during the winter with an average daily temperature of 0°C (32°F). It seems likely that an otter in the wild might require rather more food because of the energy needed to hunt successfully. On the other hand wild otters are rarely faced with a surfeit.

When an otter catches a small fish it eats all of it, but when larger specimens are taken, some bones may be left and in the case of large cyprinids the fish's pharangeal teeth are usually left on the bank surrounded by a patch of scales, and it is then possible to identify the quarry by the teeth.

The most usual way to find out what wild otters feed on is by analysis of their spraint. Otters have a relatively rapid and incomplete digestion and many small bones and scales are usually present in their spraint giving it a characteristic spiky appearance.

The bones (often only small fragments are present), scales and other fragments can be examined either with the naked eye or under a binocular microscope. Identification of fish is not easy, even with a collection of fish skeletons for reference and detailed analysis requires the ability to recognize small fragments. Often it is only possible to name with certainty the family to which the specimen belongs, unless a particular fish happens to be the only representative of its family in that particular habitat.

Feathers, mammal hair and pieces of bone or teeth from small mammals may turn up in spraint and can be identified from one of the published keys listed in Jean Webb's *Otter Spraint Analysis*. Amphibian bones are cylindrical and some have a characteristic shape which makes identification easy. A few examples of spraint analysis are shown below.

If an otter kills a large fish, as sometimes happens with salmon that are weak from spawning, it may only eat the flesh from part of the victim and when this happens little of value is likely to show up in the spraint.

Some writers have claimed that otters will eat eggs, but whole eggs were either ignored by my captive otters or were used briefly as play objects. Only if I broke open the egg would they eat the contents.

4 – Underwater world

If a fish looks upwards through the water it can see objects on land or in the air, but only if they are within an angle of about 98°. In effect the fish has a round skylight above its head and outside the area covered by this 'bubble' the water surface reflects the light and the fish sees only a mirror picture of the bottom of the river. Sight is extremely important to most fish and they can see over a field of about 330° horizontally, their clearest vision being straight ahead where a field within an angle of about 30° is covered by both eyes. A human diver lying on the bottom of the river and looking upwards can see nothing on land or in the air however clear the water. All he sees is a silvery opaque sheet like frosted glass.

In addition to excellent sight many fish have keen hearing and a well-developed sense of smell. They also have a sense of taste located in the mouth, on the underside of the head and spread over part of the body surface.

In addition to these senses, the fish has a lateral line running along each side of its body. It comprises a series of sense organs, small open tubes, connected by a duct filled with slime. The lateral line organs enable the fish to estimate very accurately the direction and distance of any disturbance in the water which sets up pressure waves. The fish can 'feel' the presence of other fish, water plants, stones or any object which enters its field of sensitivity.

An otter floating near the surface of a millpool looks down at the camera.

To human ears the silence of the underwater world is broken only by the rasping and bubbling noises of one's breathing equipment and I remember very clearly the first time I dived in a mill pool to watch one of my tame otters. Standing on the bridge looking down the water had appeared quite clear. I could see stones on the bottom and the waving beds of water moss.

Once submerged, it was more like a dull November afternoon. Visibility was a bare metre and I frequently bumped into unseen objects. The otter thought the whole business was great fun and kept materializing out of the murk to peer into my face mask. More often than not I found myself struggling through almost impenetrable tangles of pondweed and the only fish I saw were shoals of fry which scattered and quickly disappeared into the greyness.

Since that day I have dived with my tame otters many times in rivers, ponds and in the sea. When the visibility is good I am always entranced by the otter's complete mastery of its underwater world. It seems to flow through the water, turning and twisting with effortless grace. Following them day after day under all sorts of conditions I have been able to build up a picture of their underwater behaviour much of which was previously unknown or only guessed at. True my otters are not wild, but once in their natural element, free of all human ties and beyond human control, much of their behaviour, apart from their lack of fear can differ little from that of wild otters.

When swimming on the surface the otter dog-paddles with all four feet, using its tail as a rudder. It is unable to attain any speed but is able to listen and look around. Underwater the otter tucks its forepaws back close to its flanks and drives itself forward by a powerful flexing action of its rear quarters and rudder. The hindpaws may be kicked occasionally for added impetus, but the main drive comes from the otter's body and rudder, much as a whale uses its massive tail flukes in powerful vertical strokes. The otter's action beneath the surface can best be described as undulating and apparently effortless, but its

When swimming on the surface the otter dog-paddles with all four feet and is able to look around.

41

An otter dives by flexing its
body and driving itself down
by two or three powerful kicks
of its webbed hind feet.

European otter catching an eel underwater.

Otter surfacing with a fish
clasped to its chest.

OPPOSITE
Eels are the otter's favourite
quarry.

speed is considerable and I can never keep up with one of my otters however
hard I flipper.

Otters have positive buoyancy and, like humans, rise to the surface if they
stop swimming. This enables an otter to lie on the surface with its head
underwater watching all that goes on below.

Since an otter swims faster and more easily underwater its normal method
of travelling consists of a series of shallow dives, surfacing regularly to breathe.
The dive is affected by dipping its head below the surface, at the same time
flexing its body and driving itself down by two or three powerful kicks of its
webbed hind feet. The action is so smooth the animal seems to slide
downwards.

When intending to dive to greater depths the otter rolls over in a graceful
curve, its rudder following its body in a perfect arc. The action is porpoise-like
and gives the impression of great power, the body almost doubling up at the
start of the dive. Seen from below, the otter plummets straight down, air-
bubbles streaming from its coat.

Sometimes an otter will tread water with its hind paws, its body almost
vertical so that it can raise its head and neck as high as possible for better
vision. From this position the animal can apparently sink straight down
beneath the surface leaving scarcely a ripple; seen from below, the action

44

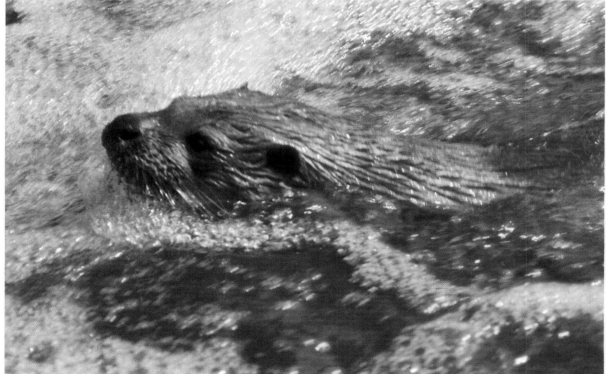

differs little from a normal dive except that the head is drawn under before the body is flexed and the hind paws kicked to provide the downward propulsion.

If alarmed when swimming on the surface the otter can crash-dive instantaneously with a mighty splash caused by the rudder hitting the water. Two otters at play, especially a courting pair, will occasionally leap completely clear of the water, often several times in quick succession like dolphins. To do this they put on a tremendous burst of speed in order to provide the momentum to keep the action going.

The pursuit and capture of moving prey is innate behaviour in the otter. I discovered this in 1965 when I fed live eels to a female North American otter and her two cubs, then three and a half months old. There was a large concrete pool in their enclosure and when I threw the eels into the water the bitch otter caught one immediately and took it ashore. One of the cubs began to chase the remaining eel which it eventually caught and ate in the normal way. It was the first time it had ever seen a live fish.

More recently I took two hand-reared European otter cubs, then four months old, to the river and donning a wetsuit I swam with them. It was the first time they had ever been in water that contained living quarry yet the boldest cub caught and ate a stickleback in the first half hour. I was very close to her at the time and watched the shoal of fish scatter at her approach before

An otter turning at speed underwater in pursuit of a fish.

OPPOSITE
Top These European otter cubs, four months old, were bred at the Otter Trust. The cubs are extremely playful both in the wild and in captivity.

Below The foaming water at the tail of a weir is a favourite place for otters to hunt for fish.

45

A dog otter turning near the
bed of the river.

darting into a thick mass of watercress. The otter followed them and began to root among the tangle of stems and shining green leaves. The fish chose to hide rather than flee and the otter easily winkled out one of them, seizing it in her mouth.

Later I was to learn that most slow-swimming fish – eels, roach, bream and gudgeon – will, if chased by an otter, try to hide in weed or among stones or boulders with the result that they are easily caught. At first I was surprised just how easy it was for an otter to catch most species of coarse fish, often by just out-swimming them, for fish, especially smallish ones, tire easily and are capable of swimming fast only in short bursts. Sometimes the otter takes its quarry in its forepaws, at the same time biting it and surfacing with the fish in its mouth, but most prey is seized in the otter's jaws. When pursuing its prey underwater the otter can turn with remarkable agility using its rudder and its webbed feet.

My otters often swim very close to the bottom of the river so that they can attack a fish from below thus achieving the advantage of surprise since fish cannot see directly downwards. Observed from above the fish in a shoal appear to lie one behind the other, but seen from the same level it immediately becomes apparent that each individual, while conforming to the general pattern adjusts its depth and distance to keep clear of its neighbour's wash or slipstream.

At the approach of an otter the shoal invariably scatters, the victim, apparently chosen at the last minute, fleeing for the nearest cover. Almost at once the remaining fish reassemble as though they know that the danger for them has passed. Herds of antelope will react in the same way to an attack by lions.

For human beings who are used to looking at the surface of the river and seeing only the reflection of the sky and the trees or at the most patches of weed in the shallows, the world beneath the surface is a new and exciting place. Baffling at first and sometimes rather sinister, it soon becomes as familiar as a well-known woodland path. As I write, the River Waveney flows silently, a stone's throw away from my home. In summer, especially after a dry spell, its unpolluted water is clear and visibility good enough for filming. I often dive with the tame otters to study their behaviour and so have come to know well the winding reaches, almost a kilometre long, bordering my land.

Whenever possible I choose bright days and swim downstream with the sun behind me. The current is slow and the river varies in depth from two to four metres in the middle so my flippers do not kick up any sediment which in shallow water would impair visibility.

The otter usually remains within sight for substantial periods as long as I keep going and do not become too engrossed in fish spotting. Even when we lose contact it returns sooner or later to see where I am.

The river shelves steeply beneath both banks, walls of shining brown mud dropping into deep water. The mirrored surface, silver bright, is broken along the edges by a frill of riverside plants. Water voles are common along this stretch and I often see one suddenly appear plopping from above in a burst of small, silver bubbles. Unlike otters, voles swim below the surface by paddling with all four feet and they usually disappear rapidly into one of the underwater entrances to their burrow.

In the shallows the sun flickers on the bright green crinkled beds of water lilies whose submerged leaves are cabbage-like and often dusted by a fine layer of silt. Fish show up well against such a pale background and clusters of small fry, minnows, sticklebacks and rudd hang suspended in the clear water. At my approach they dart this way and that, flashing sparks of silver and green.

The sun sends prongs of light stabbing down into the depths. They move ahead of me as I swim as though emanating from a light source on my head. If a cloud obscures the sun, visibility drops like a winter fog.

In the deeper reaches above the boat slipway, the sun sends shimmering bars of golden light across the pale mud where emerald green spikelets of the introduced Canadian pondweed grow as close as a lawn. In open patches small, speckled gudgeon hug the bottom, beautifully camouflaged against the mud and gravel, their protruding mouths wide open to suck in insect larvae and other minute forms of animal life carried to them by the lazy current.

Above them the floating leaves of arrowhead and water lilies lie silhouetted against the opaque ceiling of the river, anchored to the bottom by long ropes of brown tendrils through which swim shoals of silvery fish.

An avenue between the swaying stems of shining pondweed leads to an underwater garden rich in vegetation surrounding an amphitheatre of pale yellow sand. Fish of all sizes swim at every depth, a shoal of perch moves gently among the forest of stalks, their grey-green bodies striped vertically to match the translucent leaves of the pondweed. Like the otter I follow the paths between the beds of water weed. Fish are everywhere and looking down in deep water I often see the dark, thick-bodied forms of fat tench passing beneath me, keeping close to the floor of the river.

Under such conditions I have often watched one of my otters catch a fish, sometimes within a few centimetres of my face mask. I have had eels chased by an otter attempt to use my body as a refuge, something I do not enjoy as I have a horror of eels, especially large ones, though curiously I do not mind snakes, as long as I know when to expect them.

Pursued by an otter, an eel can put on quite a turn of speed, no longer swimming with its usual rather slow, sinuous movement but fleeing straight as an arrow, the lateral waggle of its tail speeded up to a blur of movement. Seen from the same level the eel looks more like a silvery-green fish and less like a water snake.

Moving water nearly always stimulates an otter to play and whenever I dive in the mill pool I make a point of swimming along the bottom to the deepest part immediately below the old red-brick road bridge where an arched culvert runs back to the sluice gate operated from within the mill itself. The water roars down the dark culvert tumbling over the sill and into the pool in a torrent of creamy-white froth. Down below, visibility is almost nil, but by lying to one side of the main current, a favourite place for the fish which live in the pool, and looking upwards, I can watch the vortex of brilliant white cloud formed by a myriad of silver bubbles where the entire volume of the river crashes down into the deeps, rolling over and over as it dashes past me, small strings of bubbles flying off the main stream like puffs of white smoke.

48

This sparkling turmoil is the otter's favourite place and I always marvel at its ability to master the torrent. I have seen it dive straight down to flash past me, its body spinning in an explosion of bubbles. Often it approaches the roughest water from below, driving itself upwards through the swirling cloud to surface below the sill only to turn and dive again allowing the force of the current to toss it downstream like a piece of driftwood.

In the clear shallows the otter searches for crayfish, turning over stones the size of bricks by forcing its muzzle beneath one side, then heaving with its head while kicking powerfully with its hind feet. Sometimes it finds a round pebble, an appealing plaything. Then it will turn on its back close to the bottom of the river and juggle the stone between its forepaws and chest. Often it loses interest before surfacing, at other times it will swim up with the stone in its paws and continue to play on the surface, dropping it and diving down to catch it again.

Much of the otter's courtship takes the form of play and mock fights both on land and in the water, sometimes above but often below the surface. I have watched two young otters indulging in such play, diving in pursuit of one another, rolling and spinning as one animal, shadow-boxing together as if floating in space, all the time surrounded by a halo of silver bubbles. When the chase takes them upwards I watch them burst through the bright ceiling of the river as they disappear into the world of sunshine leaving behind them a cloud of spent bubbles.

5 – Breeding habits

As recently as 1968, C.J. Harris wrote in the first chapter of his book *Otters* that 'Comparatively little is known about the breeding of the otter, and it would seem that the only forms to have been bred successfully in captivity are the European *Lutra lutra*, the North American *L. canadensis* and, recently, the Indian smooth-coated otter *L. (L.) perspicillata*. The first has bred twice at the London Zoo, the births taking place in August 1846 (not 1836, as stated by Zuckerman) and August 1856. In both cases two cubs were born.'

Since those words were written four species of otter have been bred at the Norfolk Wildlife Park at Great Witchingham and more recently at the Otter Trust at Earsham in Suffolk. Altogether 22 litters of cubs have been born from which 42 young otters have been reared. Eight litters of European otter *Lutra l. lutra* have been produced from which 14 cubs have been successfully reared and, in addition, a further eight litters of an Eastern race of the European otter, *Lutra l. barang*, have also been born from which eleven cubs were reared. We anticipate that more births will have occurred in both collections by the time these words are in print.

As far as we can tell no European otters were successfully bred in captivity, certainly in Britain, between that recorded by A.H. Cocks in 1881 and 1970 when the species was bred at the Norfolk Wildlife Park for the first time. Since then I have spent many hours watching the family life of the otter from shortly after the birth of the cubs until they were weaned four months later, and as a result have been able to accumulate hitherto unrecorded data.

To achieve this I provided the bitch otter with an artificial holt, the back of which consisted of a plate-glass window built into the end of a light-tight wooden hut. A photo-flood lamp, controlled by a rheostat so that the illumination could be increased slowly, enabled me to watch and film a complete record of events within the holt.

A bitch otter is believed to come into oestrus every 40–45 days and to remain so for about 14 days. It seems likely that her increased scent is carried on the current and it is certainly concentrated at her spranting places. The dog otter soon picks it up and so the two animals come together. The bitch may not be ready to mate, but the dog will keep trying until he succeeds.

I recently put two European otters together and observed them closely for more than six hours. The bitch was not fully in oestrus and at first she kept up a continual chittering which indicated that she was likely to become aggressive if approached too closely by the dog. After the first hour she 'chittered' less, but throughout the whole of this period she kept approaching and sometimes chasing the male who at the last minute always ran away from her, although apparently she did not intend to press home her attack.

Both otters spranted and scent-marked in various places and during the second hour the dog began to approach the bitch, sometimes getting quite close, only to retreat when she lunged at him. Once, when she was lying on her back in the grass, he rushed in and rolled against her on his side but jumped up and right over her before she could bite him. While doing this he moved his rudder very vigorously from side to side in a pronounced scything action. I have seen Indian smooth-coated otters and Asian short-clawed otters do this to ward off another otter approaching from behind while they were eating and it appears to be a means of defence.

During the third hour the bitch chittered even less and began bouts of exaggerated, even phrenetic, rolling and drying movements in the grass, often lying on her back and waving her front paws in the air.

During the fourth hour the two otters frequently chased each other in the water, but never made a direct approach, both sheering away at the last minute. When contact was finally made, after six hours, both animals were in the water. Thereafter they played together at intervals and ten hours from their introduction, they were sleeping peacefully in the grass about 1m apart.

Three days later the pair were seen mating in the water. Copulation was preceded by vigorous 'play', the dog chasing the bitch in and out of their pool and all over their large enclosure. At times both otters swam and dived together, twisting and corkscrewing through the water. There was also much mock fighting, the pair facing each other, submerged except for their heads and lunging at each other's faces and necks. Finally the bitch lay still on the surface, her back awash and her rudder arched and held just clear of the water. The dog mounted her from behind grasping her loins between his forepaws and gripping the back of her neck in his mouth.

Courtship play of otters below the water.

Copulation lasted 22 minutes, the pair rolling over and over sideways and sometimes disappearing below the surface. Quite short bursts of vigorous pelvic thrusts by the dog otter were separated by longer periods of rest or less vigorous thrusting.

This was fairly typical mating which I have seen many times and although it took place under captive conditions, it seems likely that much the same happens in the wild.

It is our practice to remove the dog otter as soon as the bitch appears to be pregnant, though often this is by no means easy to diagnose, especially if the bitch is carrying only one cub. In the wild the dog otter probably leaves the bitch a few days after mating to continue patrolling his territory.

The gestation period of the European otter was assumed by Cocks (1881) to be around nine weeks and our records suggest that this is correct. It is difficult to be accurate to the day since there is always a chance that a later mating taking place during the night may have gone unseen. For this reason we take into account only the actual period the two animals are in the same enclosure. This gives us a maximum and a minimum and by removing dog otters after different periods we have recorded a minimum possible gestation of 61 days, i.e. cubs were born 61 days after the dog was removed, and a maximum of 74 days, i.e. cubs were born 74 days after the pair were first placed together. Therefore we can be certain that the gestation period lies between nine and ten-and-a-half weeks.

Both dog and bitch otters will line their holts with grass, reed, water plants or other vegetation which they tear up and carry in their mouths, but bitch otters usually make a more substantial bed. Both sexes often incorporate quite thick twigs, 15 millimetres or more in diameter, which might appear to make the bed uncomfortable, but such bulky material may ensure better air circulation and therefore a drier bed. On the other hand otters do not appear to seek out dry vegetation and very often the bed is decidedly damp. Should the entrance to a holt be underwater the bedding will naturally get sodden on the way in, as it will if the otter has to swim to reach its holt.

Shortly before the cubs are born the bitch often adds considerable quantities of fresh material making a bulky nest with a hollow in the centre where she lies.

From one to four cubs may be born in a litter, though I have never known more than three, the average number being 1.7 in a total of 13 litters of Eurasian otters born either in the Norfolk Wildlife Park or at the Otter Trust. The cubs may be born in any month of the year, though in my experience there appears to be a peak in the autumn and early winter. However, the number of births recorded may be too low to be significant.

Bitch otters are able to breed in their third year while some dog otters mature earlier and I have recorded a young male only 18 months old when he fathered cubs. The youngest of our bitch otters to breed was 2 years and 2 months old when her first litter was born, while the oldest was 5 before she produced her first litter. The average age of eight of our Eurasian otters at the birth of their first litter was 3 years 8 months.

At birth the cubs are about 12 cm long including their tails and are covered with short, very pale grey fur. Their eyes are closed and their square-shaped

muzzles, small ear orifices and pads are bright salmon pink. The bitch curls her body tightly round them often sleeping with her chin resting on the base of her rudder. Whenever she moves the cubs chirrup like small birds.

Some writers have stated that bitch otters have six teats, but all those I have examined have had four. At first the cubs suckle every three to four hours. When hungry they struggle upwards through the fur of the bitch's belly searching for her teats, twittering softly until they find them. They suckle vigorously, wagging their little tails from side to side and kneading the bitch's stomach with their front paws.

Each bout of feeding lasts from 10 to 15 minutes and sometimes a cub will go to sleep still holding the teat in its mouth. After they have fed, the bitch takes each cub in turn holding it on its back between her forepaws while she licks its anal region. This not only keeps the cub clean, but stimulates it to defaecate, which it does with much tail wagging, the bitch licking up the faeces as they are voided.

For the first two weeks the cubs can scarcely crawl, their eyes do not open until they are 30 to 35 days old and by this time they can crawl, but not walk properly, and are able to hold up their heads.

The colour of their fur slowly changes to a darker grey becoming brown as they get older, while the interval between bouts of suckling gradually increases. During this period the bitch otter spends almost all her time lying with her cubs, leaving them during the night only long enough to feed herself.

When it is one month old an otter cub weighs between 700 g (1 lb 9 oz) and 800 g (1 lb 12 oz) depending on its sex, increasing to between 1075 g (2 lb 6 oz) and 1250 g (2 lb 12 oz) by the time it is two months old.

At about seven weeks of age the cubs suddenly begin to develop more rapidly and by this time they can run, although their balance is poor and their legs still weak. They also begin to eat solid food – fish – which the bitch brings to them. As soon as they are eating properly their faeces change in form and the bitch no longer licks them up. Instead the cubs begin to leave the holt to defaecate a short distance away.

By the time they are ten weeks old the cubs are eating well and are much stronger on their legs. They still suckle the bitch and continue to do so until they are at least 14 weeks old, but before then, usually at about three months or a few days earlier, they take their first swim.

Much has been written on this subject, usually stressing the point that the bitch otter has to teach, even coerce, her cubs to swim. I have watched cubs taking to the water for the first time on a number of occasions and there appear to be considerable individual differences in behaviour, not only among the cubs but between individual bitch otters. One bitch had two cubs of which one, a male, was very precocious and kept running to the water's edge, setting off on its own only to be hauled out by the scruff of its neck.

A few days ago I watched at dusk while another bitch brought her litter of three cubs, exactly 12 weeks old, to the edge of their pool. They had ventured as far on several evenings, but none of them had done more than paddle along the edge. This time the bitch slipped into the water as usual and two of the cubs, after some hesitation and running up and down on the bank, decided to follow her, swimming in the curiously uncoordinated way of all very young

OPPOSITE:
Bitch otter in her holt with two cubs four weeks old.

55

Bitch otter with cubs four
weeks old.

The bitch otter stimulates its
cub to defaecate by holding it
on its back between her
forepaws while she licks its
anal region.

Eurasian otter, *Lutra l. barang*, with cubs six weeks old born at the Norfolk Wildlife Park, Great Witchingham, in 1970.

cubs, their bodies bobbing along like corks. The third cub, lacking the courage to take the plunge ran up and down at the water's edge squeaking until its siblings returned.

I am sure bitch otters often encourage their cubs to swim, sometimes dragging them into the water, but I do not believe this is the general case. In the wild a bitch otter, disturbed while her cubs are still too young to swim, will carry them to safety in her mouth one at a time and observers seeing this may have mistakenly assumed that she was dragging the cub into the water in order to teach it to swim. On the other hand during a June heat-wave with the midday temperature around 27°c (80°F), I watched a captive bitch bring a month-old cub out of her holt, carrying it in her mouth to the edge of the pool where she dunked it several times before taking it back again – presumably to cool it down and prevent it becoming dehydrated by the heat.

By the time the cubs are four months old they follow the bitch on her fishing expeditions and soon learn to catch their own quarry. In the wild their life of wandering has begun, since by this time the bitch will frequently have moved her family to a different holt.

Although otters see very well underwater in clear conditions they are somewhat myopic on land and young cubs have very limited vision when their eyes first open, being unable to recognize objects more than three or four metres away until they are nearly three months old. Thereafter their sight improves rapidly and my tame otter cubs were able to distinguish me from a stranger at a distance of at least 20 m by the time they were four months old.

As might be expected in an animal with such sensitive ears, otter cubs rely a great deal on hearing to keep in contact with each other or with their mother,

58

both adult and young using those familiar very high-pitched squeaks often referred to as a whistle.

Little is known about the dog otter's relationship with the family, but from the many first hand accounts of a pair of adult otters being seen with young cubs in attendance, it is certain that he accompanies the family from time to time though possibly for only a day or two at a stretch. I have no evidence that the dog takes food either to the bitch or to the cubs and on the only occasion when we have left a dog otter in a large enclosure with the bitch after her cubs were born, he made no attempt to take food to them although he was seen to visit the holt. Bitch otters with young cubs are very protective towards them and the male probably keeps his distance until the cubs are well grown, and the bitch less likely to attack him.

The cubs stay with their mother until they are about one year old, although in the last two or three months of this period they become increasingly independent. When they finally leave her they probably stay fairly close to the home territory for some time before wandering away on their own. This is likely to be the most vulnerable time in an otter's life since it is exposed to numerous dangers and is compelled to range far and wide through unfamiliar country while attempting to establish its own territory, which may mean journeying to a different river or to a distant part of the coastline, since favourable territories are likely to be occupied by resident otters always ready to drive away intruders.

The comparatively long period during which otter cubs are dependent upon their mother means that a bitch can bear only one litter in a year and in practice there may be a longer interval between successive litters.

Bitch otter, *Lutra l. lutra*, with two cubs 14 weeks old bred at The Otter Trust.

59

6 – Communication

By comparison with social otters like the Asian short-clawed otter or the Indian smooth-coated otter the European otter is silent. This is to be expected, since animals which are solitary by nature do not as a rule have or need such an extensive vocabulary as those which are social. The latter are constantly reacting to other members of the group and therefore need to communicate frequently. Such communication is usually vocal, though other means may be used including visual signals, such as the raising and curling of the upper lip, bristling of the hackles and raising of the tail when two strange dogs meet.

The most well-known otter noise is the so-called whistle which, as noted earlier, is not a whistle at all but a very high-pitched and piercing squeak. That it is the most familiar vocalization is partly due to the prominence given to it by numerous writers, but also because it is the sound most likely to be heard by

Twist of grass scraped up by wild otter showing spraint deposited on top of it.

Twist of grass made by captive bitch otter. Similar twists are made by otters in the wild but the precise meaning of this behaviour is still unknown.

61

the casual observer. Young cubs are able to call loudly in this way by the time they are two months old. It is a contact call and means roughly 'I'm here. Where are you?' A pair of otters keep in contact with each other this way and cubs use it constantly whenever they become separated from the rest of the litter or from their mother. A bitch otter who has lost a cub will keep calling all the time she searches for it.

By far the commonest sound made by otters is the 'hah', a short explosive exhalation. Unlike the contact call this sound does not carry far. It is used in various ways but is basically an alarm call. A bitch otter uses it to make her cubs hide when danger threatens. An otter approaching an unfamiliar object, drawn on by its curiosity, will keep moving a few steps forward, stopping to 'hah' before retreating a few paces until it overcomes its fear.

Very young cubs 'chirrup' like small birds, but as they grow stronger the 'chirruping' gradually turns into a louder squeak which eventually develops into the high-pitched contact call.

The otter's threat call is a querulous chittering noise on a rising note and if this does not have the desired effect it turns into a scream of rage just before the animal attacks its adversary. A similar noise, though deeper in tone and quieter, indicates the same warning but at lower intensity. It is frequently made by a bitch otter when the dog begins his advances during courtship.

When a pair of otters are reunited after a period of separation they will greet each other by briefly touching noses while uttering a low 'whickering' – rather like the noise made by badgers in similar circumstances. It is quiet, friendly and confidential.

Although the facial expression of an otter does not change much, the animal is capable of other visual signs indicating its mood. The scything action of the rudder from side to side, in the face of attack from the rear has already been mentioned and is most frequently seen when one otter has food and is afraid another otter may attempt to steal it.

The opening of the mouth displaying the teeth while chittering with anger reinforces the threat of aggression. On the other hand, an otter in a friendly mood, especially during pre-courtship play, will often roll over onto its back and paw the air with its forefeet held close together.

The otter's external ears may be small but they are quite expressive and are constantly on the move, being pricked forward when the animal is listening intently and laid back when it is angry.

It seems likely that in a solitary and far-ranging animal like the otter the olfactory sense plays a major part in communication between individuals. The importance of regular sprainting sites has already been mentioned (page 29) and no doubt the anal scent glands play a major part in this means of communication.

Bitch otters sometimes produce a white, opaque jelly-like substance which has a strong musky odour. It may be deposited on top of spraint or quite separately and I have found it in the wild as well as in our otter enclosures. Its significance is not yet fully understood, but it appears to be produced when a bitch is in oestrus.

It is well known that otters make sign heaps or twists of grass, on which jelly or spraint may be deposited.

62

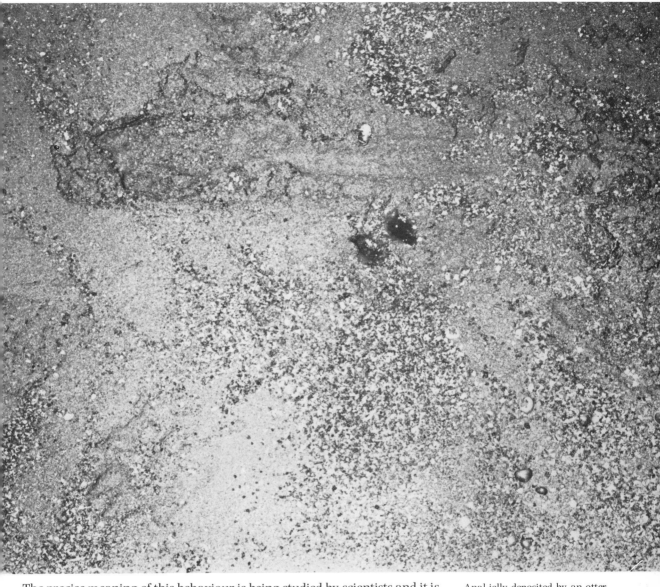

The precise meaning of this behaviour is being studied by scientists and it is not known for certain whether it can be attributed to only one or to both sexes. Quite recently we found a twist of grass made by one of our captive bitch otters and it seems likely that the practice, like the production of anal jelly, is associated with oestrus and may be a means of making the signs more conspicuous.

Dog otters are thought to produce a rather similar jelly which is usually dark in colour. The photograph shows what may be an example, with associated scraping up of the sand. The photograph was taken in the wild on a sand bar beneath a road bridge.

Anal jelly deposited by an otter (possibly a male) with sand scratched up close by.

7 – The otter and man

Over the centuries man has had a love-hate relationship with the otter, sometimes keeping it as a pet or training it to catch fish for sport, but more often condemning it to death as a marauder of the stew-pond. In modern times it has been regarded as a pest on expensive salmon and trout rivers and as a result has been trapped, shot or hunted to death.

The use of trained otters for fishing seems to have originated in China and there are many differing accounts of the method employed. The earliest reference appears to be that of a writer called Chang Tsu who lived during the Tang dynasty (A.D. 606–916) and wrote about trained otters catching fish for their owners in south China.

Other records suggest that the otters were sometimes used not to catch fish but to drive them into the fishermen's nets. In some cases the otter was tame enough to be released for its duties, but in others it was kept on a line tied tightly round its waist or to a wire collar about its neck.

A scene from an otter hunt of 1820.

London. Published by T. MᶜLean. Jan.ʸ 1. 1820

SPEARING THE OTTER

The practice of using trained otters for fishing spread to Malaysia as well as to the Sunderbunds at the mouth of the Indus and to southern India. By the fifteenth century it had reached Europe and there are accounts of trained otters in Poland, Switzerland, France and Germany. The earliest English reference, according to E.W. Gudger (1927) who researched the subject thoroughly, is in 1618 and mentions payment of £66 13s. 4d. to Robert Wood, 'Keeper of His Majesty's [James I's] cormorants, ospreys and otters'.

Few of the early writers give any indication of the way in which the otters were trained, though Freeman and Salvin touch upon the subject in their book, *Falconry*, published in 1859, when Capt. Salvin writes:

In 1848 I succeeded in taming a young otter, which I called 'Diver', so perfectly, that he would follow me into the country like a dog, and jump into my lap to sleep. At first he was an awkward swimmer, his early education being defective, owing to his separation from his parents, and I found it was necessary to be cautious with him, as cold water at first produced fits. Knowing that otters can scent fish under water, and even smell eels, etc., when in the mud, I taught him to dive by sinking meat with a plumb-line, which he never failed in finding. As the otter cannot eat a fish of any size when swimming, it must come to land to do so; its master must then approach it quietly, and taking hold of its long and strong tail (called by otter hunters 'the potter'), hold him with one hand, whilst he takes the fish from him with the other, immediately rewarding him with small pieces of fish, after which he will again take the water in search of more. Otters are particularly fond of salmon, and in some waters a great many may be taken. I need hardly remark that the death-struggle of a large salmon with his foe, in a rapid stream, is a grand and exciting thing to witness.

Provided a little sawdust or sand is placed in a corner, the otter will be found a particularly clean animal, having no perceptible smell, which cannot be said of Isaac Walton and Co. (cormorants), who indulge so much in musk, and are not very nice feeders. They are rather delicate animals, and require to be kept warm and dry, to be well fed, and kept as fat as possible. They may be fed upon both fish and flesh, such as rabbits, rats, birds, etc. Diarrhoea is a complaint to which they are liable, and their daily habit of body must be closely watched, being in a great measure an index to their health.

Knowing all too well how quickly tame otters become bored and how wilful and intractable they can be, not to mention their readiness to deliver a crushing bite if thwarted, I would hesitate before attempting to take a fish away from one. Aristotle was very nearly right when he wrote, 'The otter will bite a man, and it is said, that whenever it bites it will never leave go until it hears a bone crack.'

Whenever otters have conflicted with man's interests, man's treatment of them has been particularly violent. Otter hunting has been recognized as one of the most cruel of all blood sports, although in recent times the otter was merely hunted until, sodden and half-drowned, it was killed by the hounds. During the last century the end came when the huntsman, sometimes using a three-pronged spear like Neptune's trident, impaled the defeated creature and held it struggling above the baying pack.

In mediaeval England otters were said to have been used as turnspits, put inside a wheel similar to that in a modern hamster cage though on a much larger scale. In trying to escape the otter caused the wheel to revolve and this turned the spit through a simple system of gears. Since otters do not take kindly to captivity unless hand-reared from an early age and even then are subject to stress, the life of one used in such a manner must have been brief.

Otter meat used to be very popular in parts of Europe as recently as the beginning of the century and in Catholic countries it could be eaten during Lent since the otter lives on fish!

One kilo of otter meat is said to have cost seven to ten francs in Switzerland before the First World War (Hemmer, 1920). A variety of recipes for cooking otter meat appears in old cookery books. One such recipe advises leaving the skinned otter to soak in vinegar with lemon and bay leaves for 24 hours,

Until January, 1978, when it was banned by law, otter hunting was a popular sport.

presumably to remove any fishy flavour. The head should then be cut off and the body wrapped in buttered paper and fried with plenty of seasoning.

Otters were hunted by hounds in Europe just as in Britain and often they were given even less chance of escape, the holt being surrounded by nets in which the otter became entangled after being bolted by a terrier or a dachshund. It was then shot or stabbed to death. Variations of this form of hunting included the use of a boat in which the hunters sat with guns while the hounds scoured the river bank. Sometimes home-made explosive charges rather like squibs were employed to drive the otter from its holt.

Stew ponds were common all over Europe and Hemmer (1920) describes a cover put right over such a pond to protect the fish, which also served as an otter trap. Wooden stakes were driven into the bed of the pond to form a circular enclosure, the distance between the stakes being small enough to prevent an otter slipping through while allowing fish to pass freely. A number of funnel shaped entrances were built into the perimeter.

An otter seeing the fish within the enclosure would swim round the outside until it came to one of the entrances and could slip in. Once inside it could not find its way out again and since the enclosure was entirely covered beneath the water it could not surface to breathe and so drowned.

Traps used to catch otters included the so called bar-trap in which two toothed bars, pivoted in the form of a V, were attached to a powerful spring. To set the trap, the bars were forced apart until they lay flat on the ground. A simple trigger mechanism held them open until an otter disturbed a fine wire stretched taut across its path. This sprung the trap and the otter was crushed between the two bars.

Traps were often set in places where the otter regularly left the water and sometimes in the water if it was shallow enough. Gin traps were also used in similar situations.

Gin traps are now illegal in Britain but are probably still used on some salmon and trout rivers. The wretched otter caught in one of these devices, its leg or legs crushed, either drowns or is held in agony, until the keeper or water baliff arrives, often hours later, to club it to death. The otter is remarkably tenacious of life and there are several horrifying accounts of trapped animals breaking loose and dragging the trap with them yet still surviving for weeks or even months before finally dying.

In the course of her work on otters in the early 1950s Marie Stephens (1957) was sent a dead dog otter from Yorkshire which was accompanied by a note apologizing for its probably poor condition, but explaining that it had been at large with a trap on its foot for six days before being captured eight kilometres away.

Oliver Pike (1950) records an otter in Norfolk which survived for several months with both hind feet in a trap – yet somehow it managed to feed itself during that time.

Recent legislation makes it an offence to kill, injure or capture an otter by any means in England and Wales or to attempt to do so. But will the river keepers and their masters, the wealthy fishing syndicates, alter their ways? Perhaps hope for a change of heart lies with a new generation of enlightened young keepers and water bailiffs.

8 – Otters in captivity

Despite their obvious charm otters do not make good pets, and are not easy to keep in captivity. The purpose of this chapter is to explain how we keep and breed otters and it will also provide a general management guide to help those in charge of the captive breeding programmes, which are being set up in several European countries with the object of producing young otters for release to reinforce depleted wild populations.

Similar methods, with some adaptations, could also be used for the propagation of other endangered species of otter, such as those occurring in South America and West Africa.

Because of its nocturnal habits and its sensitivity to all forms of stress the European otter has never been popular as a zoo exhibit, and judging from available records its life span under zoo conditions has often been all too brief.

Since there is little to be gained from keeping any wild animal in captivity unless a serious attempt is made to breed it, I will describe the methods which we have developed over the last 12 years in the hope that they may prove helpful to others similarly engaged.

Otters are very active, especially at night and should be given as much space as possible. Our breeding enclosures vary in size but none is smaller than 30 m × 15 m in area and many are much larger. Ours also have the advantage of a stream running through the range of pens connecting the pools which are about 12 m in diameter and 1.5 m in depth. These pools are semi-natural having been excavated with a mechanical digger and they all contain a flourishing growth of water plants of many species, including reed, *Phragmites communis*, which the otters often use to line their holts or breeding boxes.

At the start of a dive the otter
dips its head beneath the
surface flexing its spine before
driving itself downward with
powerful thrusts of its hind
quarters.

Otters have limited jumping
ability and are unable to clear
the ground with their hind feet
by more than a few
centimetres.

Interior of breeding den showing nest material including grass, reed, sedge and twigs carried in by the otter.

At the Norfolk Wildlife Park the enclosures are of similar size, but, having no natural water supply, the pool in each pen is lined with concrete and filled from a deep bore-hole. This entails emptying and scrubbing once every week to keep the water clean.

The area of land in an enclosure should be at least four times that of the water, preferably natural turf on a free draining soil.

Otters are not only agile climbers but efficient diggers, so that the fence surrounding their enclosure should be buried in the ground to a depth of at least 0.75 m and should be not less than 1.4 m high.

We use galvanized chain link netting 2.15 m wide, 40 mm mesh and 3 mm gauge. The netting is secured to pressure-creosoted wooden posts and is fastened to a wooden rail which forms the top of the fence. A steel overhang is also fastened to this rail. The overhang is made of flat galvanized sheeting 2 m × 1 m cut lengthways down the centre making 2 sheets 2 m × 0.5 m. One of the long edges is turned down 90° to a depth of 50 mm and the other long edge is turned down to a depth of 75 mm. The sheet is secured to the top rail horizontally with the deeper edge on the inside, the shallower edge being nailed to the outside of the wooden rail. A steel bracket on every post helps to stabilize the overhang, which although only 375 mm wide, is sufficient to prevent an otter climbing out. In areas of heavy snowfall the height of the fence will have to be increased.

70

A pair of otters, when put together, may not agree at first, so we provide two wooden dens or breeding boxes in each enclosure. The boxes are made of timber 25 mm thick and have a floor area of 610 mm × 520 mm, the height at the front being 510 mm and at the back 380 mm. The sloping roof is hinged and is made of the same timber covered on the outside with flat galvanized sheeting. A wooden tunnel 180 mm square and 800 mm long, made with an angle at the centre to exclude light and draught, is attached to one of the shorter sides of the box. Natural vegetation such as reed, sedge or grass is used to line the boxes as otters do not like hay or straw and usually throw it out.

As soon as a bitch otter appears to be pregnant the dog otter is removed from the enclosure, preferably some distance away, or he may try to dig his way back and cause disturbance to the bitch.

The use of the wooden dens makes it very easy to catch and remove an otter without causing it any stress simply by fixing a hinged grid of heavy duty weldmesh to the outer end of the tunnel. The grid is closed while the otter is asleep in its den which can then be transported on a wheelbarrow to another enclosure. An alternative method of catching an otter is to put an open-ended wire cage trap at the end of the tunnel and drive the animal into it. As a last resort we sometimes catch otters in a large hand net, 750 mm in diameter, but as this causes distress and there is always the risk of injury we try to avoid using it. However, if the net is made fairly deep and of strong nylon cord, an otter needing veterinary treatment such as an injection can, in skilled hands, be caught and twisted up in the net sufficiently to immobilize it while treatment is given.

When the cubs have been born they can usually be heard squeaking, but it is wise to resist the temptation to open the lid of the den to look at them. This, or any other disturbance, may cause the bitch otter to eat them and it is safer to wait until the cubs are ten days old before having a look.

The bitch should be fed normally with as little disturbance as possible. The cubs will start to eat solid food when they are about six weeks old and from then on they should be given a special diet consisting of raw minced beef, finely diced raw fish, and the raw yolk of an egg. Once they are eating well the standard otter mix referred to below can be introduced gradually to their ration so that they are eating the same food as the adult otters by the time they are five months old. Most bitch otters much prefer the cubs' rich diet to their own and the only way to ensure that the cubs are getting any of it is to give more feed than the bitch can eat.

All our otters are fed twice each day, fish or dead day-old chicks first thing in the morning and their main meal in the evening. This consists of our basic food-mix made up as follows. Quantity for one European otter:

Fresh minced beef	907 g (2 lb)
Bran	28 g (1 oz)
Rolled or crushed oats	42 g ($1\frac{1}{2}$ oz)
Biscuit meal	84 g (3 oz)
Yeast	14 g ($\frac{1}{2}$ oz)
Heart (ox)	28 g (1 oz)
Carrot	28 g (1 oz)

The mix is made each day since it turns sour quickly. The biscuit (dog) meal is soaked before use and the final mix has the consistency of uncooked dough. Each otter has as much as it will clear up and any uneaten food is removed the following day. All feeding troughs are kept scrupulously clean.

In addition to the mix, all the otters are given fish with their evening feed, usually whiting, herring or eels, or dead day-old chicks. Herrings are never fed more than twice weekly since they are rich in thiaminase, an enzyme which destroys thiamin, part of the vitamin B complex, causing deterioration of the coat and, if fed in sufficient quantity, paralysis.

Eels are expensive, but otters are very fond of them and they are often the only food a sick otter will eat. Whenever possible we try to give fresh eels to bitch otters which have just had cubs. Some authors recommend feeding live eels to captive otters and while the otters no doubt enjoy it, the practice is illegal in Britain where only invertebrate animals may be given alive to other animals, including snakes.

When the cubs are small it is most important to keep the water level in the pool right up so that they can climb in and out easily. Steep-sided ponds, especially if made of concrete, are fatal as a cub may drown before the bitch notices its difficulty.

An otter on the saltings of the north Norfolk coast.

Eurasian otter with cubs born at the Norfolk Wildlife Park, Great Witchingham.

As cubs in the wild remain with their mother for 10 to 12 months we rarely separate them until they are at least eight months old. When the time comes we leave the bitch otter in her own enclosure and take the cubs as far away as possible, keeping the litter together for a further four to five months. If the bitch is removed to another enclosure away from her cubs she will make every effort to get back to them and is likely to lacerate her forepaws with frenzied digging or scratching at the netting. Leaving her in her accustomed pen causes far less stress.

In some cases bitch otters are given a rough time by their growing cubs which continually worry them. When this happens we part the family as soon as it becomes obvious that the bitch is losing condition and is getting little peace. By this time the cubs are always more than five months old.

The otter's habit of sprainting in the same place makes the task of keeping the enclosure clean much easier since droppings can be collected daily and the sites can be sprinkled regularly with fresh sand to keep them clean and dry.

A healthy otter has a sleek, shiny coat which sheds the water immediately the animal comes ashore. This gives it a spiky appearance at first, caused by the outer guard hairs sticking together, but the coat appears normal again and dry, as soon as the otter has rolled and rubbed itself on the ground. If, when the animal leaves the water, its coat remains smooth with a 'plastered down' effect the otter is not fit and may succumb to pneumonia as a result of getting soaked. This condition can be caused by the otter being sick or by pollution of the water by, for example, a thin layer of fish oil lying on the surface which often happens if mackerel are given as food.

OPPOSITE:
Jeanne Wayre hand-rearing an orphaned European otter cub four weeks old.

74

Otter cubs start to eat solid food when they are seven weeks old.

TOP:
After each feed the cubs slept soundly in a cardboard box.

Cubs born in the wild are particularly vulnerable when they first begin to follow their mother on her nightly fishing expeditions. When this happens they are usually at least three months old, but if the breeding holt has been disturbed the bitch may travel with her cubs to a new location when they are considerably younger and I think this is when the cubs often come to grief particularly if there are two or three in the litter and the bitch is forced to carry them one at a time across such obstacles as roads or streams.

If undisturbed she is unlikely to lose contact with any of her cubs, but those left behind while she carries one of their siblings keep up their high-pitched squeaking which attracts predators including human beings. I know of several cubs, all of them between seven and ten weeks old, which have been found in this way and picked up. Had they been left alone I am sure the bitch would have returned for them.

Young cubs 'rescued' in this way are not difficult to rear on a bottle especially once their eyes are open. They should be given Ostermilk, or some other milk substitute fed to human babies, in an ordinary feeding bottle at blood heat every three hours or so, allowing them to take as much as they want.

After each feed it is essential to wipe the cub's face and mouth with a damp towel to remove surplus milk. It is also necessary to stimulate it to defaecate by massaging its anal region with a wad of warm wet cottonwool.

Between feeds cubs less than six weeks old are best kept warm, but not hot, on a bed of soft clean straw in the bottom of a large, deep cardboard box. If the cub is about two months old when found it should weigh about 1135 g ($2\frac{1}{2}$ lbs) and at this age it will probably refuse to have anything to do with milk or a bottle and will require feeding with finely diced raw fish, especially eels, minced raw beef and yolk of egg. At first it should be left alone as much as possible, but kept reasonably warm and dry in a hutch or box well lined with clean straw or hay and attached to a small pen containing a shallow dish of fresh, clean water. The cub will probably eat during the night when there is no disturbance.

If kept under good conditions, and adequately fed and cared for, otters are not susceptible to many diseases, but are prone to accidental bites when playing together and if not treated at once these are likely to become septic. Usually treatment by broad-spectrum antibiotics given either by sub-cutaneous injection or orally over a period of several days will prove effective.

In common with most animals in captivity otters are susceptible to internal parasites including both roundworms and tapeworms although their occurrence is not frequent and both are readily controlled by modern drugs.

Dental abscesses are quite common in otters in captivity and possibly in the wild, and are difficult to cure except by the use of antibiotics or by veterinary treatment which may necessitate the removal of an infected tooth or surgery to drain the abscess.

Otters in captivity are also susceptible to leptospirosis or Weil's disease, a virus carried by rats, mice and other rodents. It usually strikes without warning and is fatal so it is essential to prevent rats from entering otter enclosures. Small mesh wire-netting (12 mm) on the outside of the chain-link fencing, buried at least 300 mm in the ground with a band of flat galvanized steel sheeting along the top of the pen 300 mm in depth will prevent entry by rats so long as they are not permitted to burrow underneath. Rats are best controlled by a combination of regular baiting outside the enclosures with the poison given in plastic drain piping, 75 mm in diameter cut into 450 mm lengths, to keep the bait dry and Fenn traps set in wooden tunnels at intervals along the outside of the pens.

A vaccine against leptospirosis is available for use in dogs, but as far as I know it has not been tried on otters. There have also been reports of otters in captivity contracting canine distemper and pneumonia. The former is unlikely to occur if no dogs are allowed near the pens and the latter is usually caused by mismanagement resulting in the otter suffering from exposure.

9 – Otter conservation

The general decline in the numbers of otters not only in Britain but over the whole of Western Europe has been so drastic that in most countries the otter is now protected by law. In England and Wales it has recently (1 January 1978) been added to Schedule I of the list of animals protected under the 1975 Conservation of Wild Creatures and Wild Plants Act, and if the law is observed it should go a long way towards stopping a further decline.

The effect that the new Order will have on otter hunting is not yet known since only the courts can decide if hunting is legal or illegal so long as the huntsman claims he is not attempting to kill or injure the otter. Britain must be one of the few countries in the world where such a farcical situation could exist and already (March 1978) there have been reports in the press that some packs of otter hounds intend to continue to hunt, but that in future their quarry will be mink or coypu.

Since it is impossible for a huntsman to know for certain what line his hounds are hunting until the quarry is driven into view the chance of hunting an otter will not be diminished and the disturbance to the otter and the stress inflicted upon it will be just as damaging. Even if not illegal nobody could suggest that this would be within the spirit of the law. Only time will tell what the final outcome will be.

The otter is not yet protected in Scotland because its numbers there are thought to be satisfactory. Jim Green has recently started a two year national survey in that country and when repeated in, say, ten years' time it will give an indication of any change in the population level. Scotland, particularly the west coast, has what is probably the most important surviving population of otters in Western Europe and it is unfortunate that under existing legislation nothing can be done to protect it until the animal has become so rare that its future is in danger and by then it may be too late.

The precise cause of the otter's decline is not known, though it seems certain that pollution of rivers and lakes by sewage effluent, the waste products of industry and agricultural chemicals has played an important part. The activities of the Water Authorities including the cutting of bankside vege-tation, the felling of trees, weed cutting and in some areas the killing of water plants by herbicides, have all accelerated the otter's disappearance from many of its former haunts, while the increased use of waterways for recreation, fishing, boating and walking and the draining of marshes for agriculture have resulted in further loss of habitat. Add to all these factors the killing of otters in the past by hunting and by trapping and shooting in the interests of fishery protection, and it is easy to understand why the European otter is now in danger of extinction.

Since loss of habitat is probably the most important single factor in the

An otter at the tail of the weir.

otter's decline it follows that only a concerted effort by governments, landowners and naturalists to halt this destruction can save the otter.

Regrettably the policy of the Ministry of Agriculture in Britain appears to be to drain all low-lying areas as quickly as possible in order to convert them to arable farming in the cause of greater cereal production. This is understandable in a world where four-fifths of the human population is undernourished. But it should be remembered that, in common with some animals, human beings tend to multiply in direct ratio to the available food supply.

It is a sobering thought that if our agricultural masters have their way there will not be a single lowland grazing marsh left in Britain by the end of this century. The wetlands and all the life they support, including the otter, will have gone for ever and in their place bleak fields of sugar beet, barley and potatoes will lie divided by rivers as straight and bare-banked as Dutch canals.

The farmers are not entirely to blame for this state of affairs. They are businessmen operating in a competitive market and subject to heavy taxation. If they are to survive they have to adopt modern, intensive methods which take no account of landscape or wildlife conservation.

It is time to develop a national land use strategy in which it is recognized that wildlife and landscape are just as important objectives as food and timber production. If farmers are to protect wildlife habitat such as hedgrows, woods and marshes, it must become official policy to encourage them and worthwhile fiscal incentives must be offered. It is unrealistic to expect farmers to respond to the needs of conservation unless they have the country's backing and know that they will not suffer financially.

Fortunately the need to resolve the opposing aims of agriculture and conservation has been recognized by the Nature Conservancy Council in the publication of a paper entitled *Nature Conservation and Agriculture* (1977), and concludes (Para. 54) that 'a national policy would ensure that as an individual he was not financially penalized for doing what was best for the nation in the long term. In general terms, a rural land use strategy would encourage farmers to increase productivity by improving yields on the existing crop lands rather than by reclaiming those wildlife habitats whose value, from the national point of view, is greater for conservation than for intensive agriculture.' It is to be hoped that future governments will ensure a balance that will improve the environment for the benefit of everyone.

Recent years have seen an enormous upsurge in leisure pursuits of all kinds in the countryside and especially on our waterways. More people have taken to sailing, canoeing, motor boating, water-skiing, angling or even just walking by the river, and all this has resulted in an intolerable degree of disturbance to the otter. Nobody in their senses would suggest that this kind of pressure will not increase still farther. People have a right to enjoy themselves and whenever possible fresh waterways should be opened up for sailing, angling and other pursuits as long as the reasonable requirements of conservation are not overlooked.

There have been suggestions that there should be restrictions on boating and angling and even on public access where otter havens or sanctuaries have been established. But even if such measures were morally defensible, which they are not, they would be impossible to implement without drastic changes in the law. Thus it follows that the future of the otter lies largely in the upper and narrower reaches of lowland rivers which are generally privately owned. In such cases there is usually no public access, little or no boating and the fishing is privately controlled. It is to the landowner that we must look for the survival of the otter over large areas of Britain.

The practice of establishing otter havens on rivers started in Holland where results are said to have been encouraging. The idea is that particularly favourable stretches of a river should be declared strict or maximum security havens (M areas) in which ideally there will be no boating or angling, no public access and where bankside vegetation is allowed to flourish and weed cutting and other management practices are reduced to the bare minimum. It is hoped that otters will use these havens as places in which to lie up or breed.

Where possible the maximum security havens are linked by less strictly controlled areas where otters are still protected, but where there may be limited angling and boating and public access confined to one bank. These are known as protection or P areas. It is obvious that otter havens can be set up only with the cooperation of the landowners concerned, the local Water Authority and in many cases the anglers. Fortunately, such cooperation is possible and the Otter Trust has recently demonstrated how effective that cooperation can be. With the help of landowners, anglers, the Anglian Water Authority and the War Office (on the River Wissey), the River Waveney in Norfolk is virtually one large otter haven from its source in Redgrave Fen down to Bungay which, with its tributaries, totals approximately 60 km, of which 30 km are M areas, and 29 km are P areas. It has not been possible to trace the landowners on the remaining 1.2 km.

Thanks to the same cooperation the Otter Trust has achieved similar results on the River Wissey in Norfolk. This is also virtually one continuous otter haven from its source to below Oxborough where it has been canalized by the Water Authority and is unsuitable for otters. The total distance, with tributaries, is 39 km of which 23 km are M areas and 14.4 km P areas. Once again it has not been possible to trace the owners of the remaining 2 km. The Trust plans to continue this work, not only in East Anglia but over a much wider area of Britain.

In addition to peace and security the otter needs an adequate food supply and sufficient cover and it is often lack of cover which spoils an otherwise suitable stretch of river. When setting up havens we have found that owners will usually permit planting schemes on their land which will do much to improve the habitat. Trees such as willow, *Salix* and alder, *Alnus glutinosa*, interspersed with patches of bramble, *Rubus fruticosus*, and blackthorn, *Prunus spinosa*, will in time grow into impenetrable thickets in which otters will feel secure.

Artificial holts constructed in the river banks were popular with otter hunters years ago and more recently their use has been recommended in conjunction with otter havens. Having no experience of them I prefer to keep an open mind, though I do not understand their necessity. I have frequently watched one of my otters digging a holt in a bank and have always been surprised by the speed with which it is accomplished. The otter often disappears from view in less than half an hour, so that under most conditions a new holt could be excavated easily in a single night.

Why then did the otter hunts take the trouble to build artificial holts? I assume there were two reasons, firstly they knew where to look for an otter and secondly it was much easier to make the otter bolt from an artificial holt, which usually had a removable stone slab over the sleeping chamber, than to force one out from a natural holt secure beneath the roots of a large tree which often meant using a terrier to bolt the otter.

We intend to experiment with artificial holts in some of the otter havens we have established and we shall keep careful records of the use made of them by otters. I am indebted to Richard Barrett for the following description and sketches of the type of artificial holt which has been used with success in Shropshire.

The tunnels are made from unglazed pipes 300 mm in diameter and are roughly four metres long from the river bank to the breeding chamber, which is made of concrete blocks with an inspection slab over the top. It appears that hunts often built artificial holts with much longer tunnels, up to 14 m. These have the advantage of enabling the breeding chamber to be built well above high water level with only a gentle slope on the tunnel.

The entrances should point downstream to prevent flood debris blocking them. One should be at normal water level, the other rather higher up the bank to allow for winter flooding.

The floor of the breeding chamber must be free draining so that the otters can lie warm and dry. Concrete is useless as urine and condensation will accumulate making the chamber unusable. Heavy gauge galvanized netting, 25 mm diameter mesh, is the easiest to use and should be cemented into the foundations of the side walls to hold it securely in place, then covered with a layer of dry earth.

The breeding chamber should be sited as far above water level as possible to prevent it from becoming flooded in winter. This means choosing a place where the river bank is fairly high. If possible the tunnels should emerge beneath the cover of bushes or other vegetation.

After completion the whole site should be levelled and grassed over to cover all traces of the holt since secrecy is vital if otters are to use it in safety. The proximity of a weir or mill pool is an advantage as it means good fishing is close at hand should a bitch otter use the holt for breeding.

From time to time Water Authorities, or the River Commissioners on navigable waters, have to undertake large scale engineering works, which often leave the river bank devoid of vegetation and wildlife. Sometimes dredging and piling take place on long stretches of river which become permanently unsuitable for otters. When this happens it is important to maintain and improve alternative habitats close to the main waterway. Small tributaries and dykes should be kept overgrown and undisturbed. Reed beds, flooded gravel pits and islands with vegetation are all important and should be carefully protected and left undisturbed.

Inland Drainage Boards are renowned for their lack of consideration towards conservation or towards anything else other than the needs of agriculture. Unfortunately, the Boards, which are statutory bodies, work independently of the Water Authorities and are mainly responsible for land

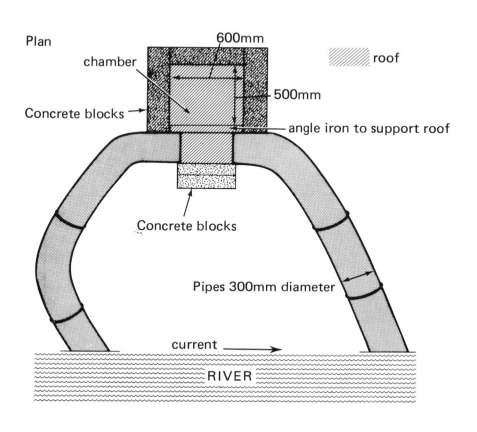

Plan

600mm

chamber

roof

Concrete blocks

500mm

angle iron to support roof

Concrete blocks

Pipes 300mm diameter

current

RIVER

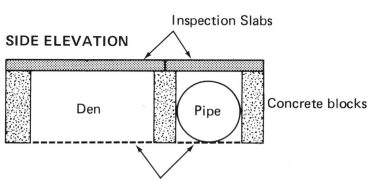

Inspection Slabs

SIDE ELEVATION

Den

Pipe

Concrete blocks

Floor — covered by galvanised wire netting
25mm mesh 16 gauge — set below blocks
forming wall and cemented round edges.

drainage away from main rivers. This means that they control huge areas of potential otter habitat. Their sole aim seems to be to get water into the rivers and so to the sea as quickly as possible and it is not unknown for them to use herbicides to destroy water plants and all other forms of life in drainage ditches and dykes. Only the landowners and farmers can redress the balance by allowing small streams and some dykes to become overgrown thus providing seclusion and cover not only for otters but for many other forms of wildlife.

Some of the huge new man-made reservoirs start off by having little or no cover round their shores while in others, particularly in the uplands, there is insufficient food to support a permanent population of otters. There is nearly always considerable disturbance on reservoirs from boating and fishing, but on those where sufficient food is available, planting close to the shore will provide suitable habitat for otters especially if public access to certain parts of the reservoirs is prohibited. This has already happened on some of the new reservoirs, such as Rutland Water, where some areas are maintained as wildlife reserves.

Water quality is all important and is the responsibility of the local Water Authority. It is known that the excessive enrichment of water from sewage outfalls and the run-off of agricultural fertilizer used on the land have a damaging effect on freshwater ecosystems, resulting in less food for otters in the form of fish and frogs. In severe cases toxic chemicals may poison the otters, in less severe instances they reduce the fish populations upon which the otters feed.

There have been reports, particularly from Scotland, of otters being caught and drowned in fyke nets. These nets originated in Holland and are now widely used by commercial eel fishermen in Britain. The net is cylindrical in design and consists of several compartments each of which has a funnel shaped entrance. When set there is also a length of vertical netting running up to the outer funnel entrance. Its purpose is to deflect fish towards the trap. At present, the entrance to a fyke net is large enough for an otter to swim through, but if it were covered with wire or strong netting with a maximum mesh size of 80 mm there would be no chance of otters getting caught and drowned.

Such a minor modification does not seem likely to diminish the effectiveness of the fyke net and I hope that before long it will become obligatory for all fishermen using these nets.

There has been much speculation in recent years on the effect of feral mink on the otter population. It has even been suggested that mink kill otter cubs, but so far there appears to be no evidence to support this claim. In my experience bitch otters are loath to leave young cubs for long and are extremely aggressive in their defence. It is a general rule of nature that little predators keep away from big predators and an otter would have no difficulty in killing a mink. Nor does there seem to be any evidence that mink have a direct effect on otter numbers by competing for the available food. However, the effect of mink, if any, on the recovery in the status of the otter is not known and more research into the subject is needed.

In common with badgers and other animals, otters are run over by cars from time to time and this usually happens at places where the otters' traditional path is crossed by a road, resulting in regular casualties. One such site is near the mouth of the River Glaven just outside Cley in Norfolk. There the river bifurcates and each channel passes beneath the main coast road via sluice gates. During the past two decades, several otters have been killed at night when forced to leave the river and cross the road to reach the coastal marshes which form an important part of their territory.

The Otter Trust in conjunction with the Norfolk Highway Authority has recently installed the first two otter underpasses to be built in this country, one beside each of the Glaven's channels. They consist of concrete pipes, 330 mm in diameter, placed close to one side of the channel a little above average water level and passing one metre below the surface of the road. Otters usually find it hard to resist exploring tunnels in the form of culverts and drains so we hope these underpasses will prove effective. If they do, the Trust intends to install more at other vulnerable places.

10 – Looking for otters

Perhaps its elusiveness makes the otter such an interesting animal to study in the wild for it represents a challenge and the successful otter-watcher has to be not only knowledgeable, but patient and determined. The chance of seeing an otter in daylight is remote except in a few favoured localities.

What then is the point of looking for otters at all? Perhaps the answer lies partly in the difficulty of getting to grips with such an elusive creature and partly in the satisfaction of finding out just a little more about its life in the wild. Our knowledge of the otter population of this country is full of gaps which need filling and that can be done only by thorough and painstaking fieldwork.

We know that in most parts of England and Wales the otter is rare or possibly non-existent, but even in more suitable areas, like East Anglia and parts of the West Country, we have no accurate population figures though scientists like Macdonald and Mason (1976) have, as a result of their surveys, arrived at an estimated figure of 34 for the number of otters in Norfolk which may prove very close to the actual number. In the same way West (1975) has carried out population surveys in Suffolk and has reached an estimated figure of 36 for that county. In the majority of other areas no detailed surveys have yet been undertaken, although at the present time workers like Elizabeth Lenton and Jim Green are attempting to gain a more general picture of the otter population in Britain as a whole.

An occupied otter's holt in woodland close to a Scottish sea loch.

Quite apart from population surveys a detailed study of one particular area or river can yield information on the behaviour of otters in the wild, a field of study which naturalists are just beginning to investigate seriously in the UK.

Nobody knows for certain how large a territory an otter needs in different kinds of habitat, or what exactly happens to adolescents after they have left their mother's care. Practically nothing is known of the effect on otters of such activities as fishing or boating, or how often each otter patrols its entire territory, or what part the dog otter plays in bringing up the family. The answers to these and many more questions are there to be discovered by the dedicated otter-watcher.

While otters are difficult to see, their signs are not and it is by these that the naturalist can assess their numbers and if he studies a given area with sufficient care and over a long enough period, can build up a picture of their nightly activity.

Some types of habitat are much easier to work in than others. Fast-flowing boulder-strewn streams and the rocky shores of remote sea lochs do not usually present much of a problem. Otters like to spraint on prominent boulders or rocks and their tracks are fairly easy to discern amongst the sparse vegetation. Their holts are often among rocks or under the roots of a tree some distance from the water, but as a rule they are not difficult to locate. Otters in such areas are often less shy and therefore easier to study.

Lowland rivers and marshes, including salt marshes along the coast are far more difficult to work. The marshes, both fresh and salt, add a new dimension with their network of drainage channels, ditches and dykes sprawling over a wide area, all of which has to be covered with the same diligence. During the summer the vegetation is often very lush, particularly near the water, making sprainting places and runs very difficult to find.

In East Anglia coypu runs and platforms add to the confusion while in other parts of the country feral mink can cause problems. The tracks of an otter in sand or soft mud are easy to recognize and should not be confused with those of coypu, mink, rabbits, rats or any other creature likely to be found in the same habitat. Illustrations of their tracks for comparison are shown below.

The tracks of some of the different creatures most frequently encountered when looking for otters. **A** Otter. **B** Coypu. **C** Mink. **D** Rabbit and **E** Brown rat.

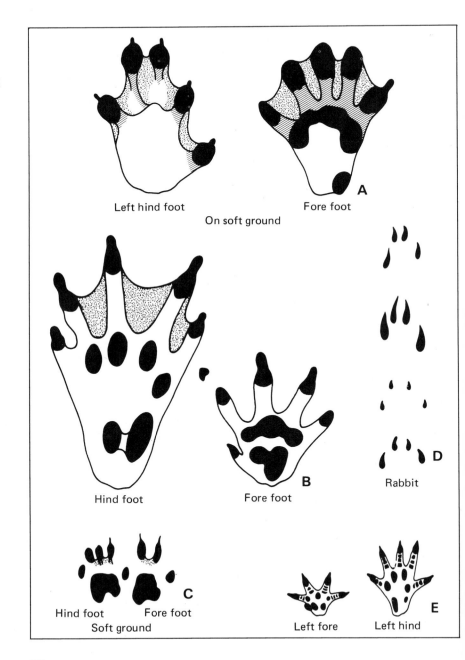

Left hind foot   Fore foot   **A**

On soft ground

Hind foot   Fore foot   **B**   Rabbit   **D**

Hind foot   Fore foot   **C**

Soft ground   Left fore   Left hind   **E**

Tracks made by an otter in
deep snow.

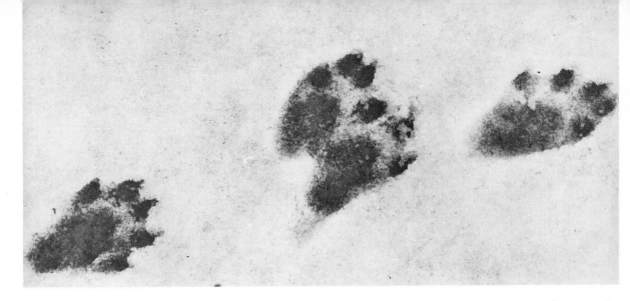

Otter tracks in snow.

Under good conditions an otter's tracks are easy to recognize because the webbing between the toes gives them a rounded appearance. The claws may or may not show as very small points depending on the consistency of the substrata. In practice it is not always easy to distinguish between the tracks of a forefoot and that of a hindfoot unless the mud or sand is just firm enough to give a perfect imprint, when the slightly larger size and increased length of a hindfoot will show.

When walking an otter places the hindfoot behind the track of the forefoot and when trotting the hindfoot usually falls on or close to the track left by the forefoot. The otter's normal gait on land is a kind of lope or canter and there is great variation in its tracks, but if moving fast the track of the hindfoot falls in front of that left by the forefoot. These tracks often appear more or less in pairs.

In theory it should be possible to get some idea of the sex, or in the case of cubs, the age of the animal making the track, but in practice so much depends on the consistency of the surface over which the animal is moving as well as its speed, which affects the weight put on each foot, that measurements can only provide the roughest guide.

The otter's normal gait is a kind of lope or canter.

On a forefoot, you will need to measure A to A, B to B and C to C. The final shape resembles a square, though slightly longer than wider.

To show this I had some areas of soft mud laid in our otter enclosures and then took a series of measurements of forefeet only. Here it should be noted that more often than not the 'thumb' does not show, resulting in a four-toed track. All the measurements were taken as shown in the above figure, with the following results giving the range and average for five individual otters.

	No. of prints measured	Range	Average
Adult			
AA	3	61 mm–57 mm	64 mm
AB	3	50 mm–57 mm	54 mm
AC	2	58 mm–66 mm	62 mm
Adult ♀ 1			
AA	7	52 mm–59 mm	55 mm
AB	9	52 mm–63 mm	56 mm
AC	2	63 mm–68 mm	65 mm
Adult ♀ 2			
AA	6	43 mm–49 mm	45 mm
AB	6	40 mm–56 mm	49 mm
AC	4	49 mm–61 mm	57 mm
Cub 16 weeks ♂			
AA	6	34 mm–47 mm	38 mm
AB	6	39 mm–47 mm	43 mm
AC	2	47 mm–51 mm	49 mm
Cub 16 weeks ♀			
AA	6	48 mm–54 mm	51 mm
AB	6	46 mm–53 mm	49 mm
AC	—	—	—

It is interesting to note that female 1 left on average a wider print than the adult male, which was almost twice her weight, while the female cub 16 weeks old left a print with the same average width as that of adult female 2.

Remains of fish killed and
eaten by an otter close to the
edge of the river.

Sprainting places have already been described and the experienced field
worker will know almost by instinct where to look. Sills or sandbars beneath
bridges are favourite sites and usually fairly easy to reach. Bridges have the
great advantage in that they can often be approached by car thus enabling the
worker to cover a large stretch of river in a single day, although the result will
of course be superficial unless the same bridges are visited regularly, preferably
weekly, over a long period.

92

On many rivers the bridges are not suitable and the only way to find out if otters are present is to walk the banks carefully searching every likely spot. This is time-consuming, tiring and frequently disheartening work, but if otters are present their signs will eventually be found and by regular observation it should be possible to deduce each individual otter's territory.

When checking bridges, a distance of 300 metres upstream and downstream of the bridge should also be examined for spraint, footprints, fish remains, sign heaps or twists of grass, slides or any other clues.

If there are boulders in the river, check the largest on which an otter could easily climb since they are nearly always favoured as sprainting places because they are less liable to inundation during a spate.

When walking the banks of a lowland river look for signs of a path or a run across any promontory and wherever the river makes a sharp turn, since an otter will usually take a short cut across land rather than swim all the way round.

Ledges on the bank and low places close to the water's edge, especially muddy cattle bays where the animals go down to drink, should be carefully examined for signs of spraint, fish remains or footprints. Otters are always attracted by weirs and frequently have a sprainting place close by. All caves in the bank and hollow trees, especially fallen ash or alders, are worth examining for the presence of a holt.

RECORDING OBSERVATIONS

Once signs have been found, especially sprainting sites, they should be marked on an Ordnance Survey map, scale 1:50,000 (1 square to 1 kilometre approximately or $1\frac{1}{4}$ in. to 1 mile) and the site named or numbered and recorded with the National Grid reference numbers.

Under the Ordnance Survey the country is divided into 100 km squares, each having a two letter code by which it can be identified. In addition the maps (1:50,000) are further subdivided into one-kilometre squares.

To give the grid reference of a site first find the grid letters from the key printed at the side of the map, then take the west edge of the kilometre square in which the site lies and read the large figures printed opposite this line on the north or south margins of the map. In order to be exact, estimate the tenths eastwards to the site. So far the figures might read, for example, TG 495. Now take the south edge of the kilometre square in which the site lies and read the large figures printed opposite this line on the west or east margins of the map. Once again estimate the tenths northwards to the site. The final figure will appear something like this: TG 495 046.

Much time will be saved by recording sites in this way and they can then be visited regularly so that a picture of the otter's behaviour can be gradually pieced together.

I am indebted to Dr D.J. Jefferies of the Nature Conservancy Council for permission to reproduce (with slight amendment) the form which he devised for the use of scientists engaged in surveying otter populations in Britain. We have included it in this book for the benefit of those enthusiasts who wish to make a serious study of the otter population in their particular area. Others may find it useful to know what scientists are doing in this field.

A								
1 Note no:					**2 Site Names:**		**3 Grid Reference**	
B								
1 Recorders			**2 County:**		**3 Altitude:**		**4 Date of Visit:**	

C HABITAT TYPE	Sea Coast	Sea Loch	Estuary	Lowland Lake/Broad	Upland Loch/Tarn	Reservoir	Running Water	Bog/Marsh	Carr	
D SHORE TYPE	Boulders	Stones	Gravel	Sand	Silt	Earth	Rock Cliffs	Earth Cliffs		
E CURRENT	Rapid	Fast	Slow	Sluggish	Static					
F WIDTH	<1m	1 – 2m	2 – 5m	5 – 10m	10 – 20m	20 – 40m	>40m			
G MEAN DEPTH	<0.5m	0.5 – 1m	1 – 2m	2 – 3m	3 – 5m	>5m				
H VEGETATION	Bankside Trees	Bankside Vegetation	Emergent	Floating Attached	Free Floating	Submerged				
J LAND USE BORDING	Upland Grassland	Permanent/Temp Grassland	Mixed/Broadleaf Woodland	Conifer Woodland	Acid Peat Bog	Arable	Salt Marsh	Heath	Urban/Industrial	Garden	Fen
K BANK TREATMENT	Canalised	Maintained	Wild							
L WEED CONTROL	Mechanical	Chemical	None							
M OTHER USE	Water Abstraction	Boating/Powered	Boat/Sail	Boat/Manpower	Bank/Angling	Bankside/Shooting	Keepered	No Use	Reserve	

N POLLUTION UNPOLLUTED

DOMESTIC		AGRICULTURE				INDUSTRIAL		
Organic	others	organic	pesticide	fertilizer	organic	toxin	solid	temperature

P	MINK SIGNS	Present
		Absent
Q	OTTER/MINK/COYPU HUNTING	Yes
		No
R	FISH (Species present)	
S	APPARENT DISTURBANCE FACTOR	

Description or sketch of site

Distance surveyed

Description or sketch of spraint site	Otter signs seen (and number)
	Salmonid ova in spraint

The general use of this form by all naturalists studying their local otter populations would ensure uniformity and therefore comparable data which would be especially useful for determining population trends through repeat surveys at a later date. It would also provide much needed information on the precise habitat preferred by otters and the effect on them of various adverse factors.

A form should be filled in once for each site and this is done by completing the horizontal columns lettered A–S either by entering the relevant information or by ticking the appropriate box. A few hints on filling in the form may be helpful. Under A and B fill in information required, under C tick appropriate box. Under D the following measurements apply:

Boulders	above 30 cm max diameter
Stones	5–30 cm max diameter
Gravel	4 mm–5 cm max diameter
Sand	0.1 mm–4 mm max diameter
Silt	predominantly inorganic material below 0.1 mm

The current (E) can be gauged by throwing a stick into the river and timing its progress.

Rapid	fast flow with broken water
Fast	greater than 1 metre per second with a smooth flow
Slow	0.1 to 1.0 m/sec
Sluggish	less than 0.1 m/sec but still a visible current

The width (F) is the visual estimate on pacing a bridge.

The average depth (G) is at the centre of the river and can be obtained by using a pole or weighted line and taking the average of several measurements. This may have to be done from a boat. If this is not possible enter probable limits with an 'S' for subjective, e.g. S3–6 m.

Under (H) vegetation:

Bankside trees	*Alnus, Salix, Populus,* etc.
Bankside vegetation	enter *Rubus, Conium, Carex,* etc.
Emergent	enter plants with base in water, *Glyceria, Phragmites, Typha,* etc.
Floating attached	*Nuphar, Potamogeton, Sagittaria,* etc.
Submerged	*Callitriche, Elodea,* etc.

British Water Plants, a key by Haslam, Sinker and Wolseley, available from the Field Studies Council (Field Studies 1975, 243–351), is very useful for identifying water plants.

Columns J to N are completed by ticking the appropriate box, while in column P simply cross out whichever is not applicable. The fish species (R) can be ascertained from local anglers or from the Water Authority. The disturbance factor (S) is a case for subjective grading from 0 (practically none) to 5 (very high, e.g. much boat traffic, walking by public).

The description of the site can usefully include a sketch and any other information not included on the form.

ANALYSING SPRAINT

The diet of otters in the wild can be determined by a careful examination of the food remains in their spraint, though to do this accurately requires a binocular microscope, considerable knowledge of fish bones and scales and preferably a reference collection of fish skeletons. It is really a job for the professional scientist rather than the naturalist.

A great deal of work on spraint analysis has already been carried out by scientists so there seems little point in further duplication, especially as the collection of spraint may very well cause unwelcome and unnecessary disturbance to the otters. For the enthusiast with the necessary skill and facilities or for those with a special reason for collecting spraint, the Mammal Society has published the excellent booklet *Otter Spraint Analysis*, written and illustrated by Jean Webb.

SIGHTING OTTERS

Once the nightly movements of otters on a river are known it should be possible to catch a glimpse of one by sitting quietly at a good vantage point. This requires a great deal of patience and as it is usually impossible to be sure when an otter will pass by a given spot in its territory the observer may have to sit up all night for a good many nights before being rewarded.

Since otters have such remarkable hearing the watcher must remain silent and preferably alone, nor must he doze since that is just the time the otter will choose to pass by. Activity is usually at a peak during the early part of the night, then falling off, but rising to another peak just before dawn.

Watch can be kept from a car if it is possible to get close enough to the river in a likely place, and it is certainly more comfortable and often warmer than being in the open. A hide, preferably wooden and permanent, is a luxury, but otters may take several months to become accustomed to a new object on the bank and if they have to pass it are likely to do so submerged or by making a detour.

If you are lucky enough to discover a breeding holt resist the temptation to put a hide near it or even to watch it at all from close by; to do so will certainly disturb the bitch otter and she will move her cubs to a safer place.

Fortunately there are still a few places especially on the west coasts of Ireland and Scotland, where the patient and silent watcher may be rewarded by the sight of an otter fishing the incoming tide in broad daylight. When that happens the cold and uncomfortable hours spent in vain are quickly forgotten.

Example of otter spraint or
droppings.

Male European otter in a
millpool on the River Wensum
in Norfolk.

99

11 – The Otter Trust

Such was my interest in otters that in 1971 I formed the Otter Trust, a registered charity whose main aims are to promote the conservation of otters throughout the world, to breed them in captivity both for scientific study and for reintroduction to the wild and to carry out field studies in order to collect scientific data to help in the management and conservation of otters.

As described in a previous book (*The River People*, 1976) an adverse planning decision forced me to sell the first property I had purchased for the Trust in Suffolk and it was not until 1975 that my wife and I were able to acquire River Farm at Earsham, near Bungay, on the border of Norfolk and Suffolk.

We realized from our first visit, or to be more accurate, Jeanne realized, that River Farm was ideal for our purpose. The River Waveney, dividing Norfolk from Suffolk, forms our southern boundary, looping round two marshes which sweep away from the Elizabethan farmhouse. The road at the end of our drive used to be the main carriageway from Bungay to Harleston. Narrow and winding it was replaced a few years ago by a wide highway on the line of the old railway track to the north, leaving our small road quiet and deserted.

The 14 hectares of land includes an attractive lake of 1.5 hectares and two spinneys, while the general layout has enabled us to keep the house, where we live, and the three hectares or so surrounding it, separate from the Trust's headquarters and otter breeding enclosures. Not least among its advantages is the distance from Great Witchingham – 50 kilometres, which allows us to continue to run our Norfolk Wildlife Park where so many of the Trust's otters were born.

The headquarters of the Otter Trust at Earsham, near Bungay, Suffolk. The Trust was opened to the public in September 1976.

We took possession on 1 October 1975, but were away in America at the time, returning on 9 October. Two days later a JCB excavator on caterpillar tracks, with a seven-metre boom, lumbered down the ramp of a low-loader and crept like a prehistoric monster across the marsh, stopping at the side of the drainage channel which runs through the middle of our land. Untouched for decades the stream had silted up and was little more than a shallow depression where sedges, reed and water celery flourished.

My idea was to construct the otter breeding enclosures in a long line with the stream running through all of them and to form a pool in each pen by digging out its banks. The excavator roared into life opening the steel jaws on its bucket to rip up mouthfuls of dripping earth and vegetation which it dropped neatly on the marsh behind it. As it worked the peaty soil shook like jelly and brown liquid swirled in the ever widening channel, for the water table was less than 60 centimetres below ground level.

Its output was phenomenal and by the end of the first day three pools were completed. I did not know that soft ground would later cause delays from bogging down. It took four weeks to complete 21 pools, the black bank of dripping soil, higher than a man, growing longer each day. Our plan was to use the soil, when it dried out, to form a raised walk-way right along the front of the enclosures so that visitors would not have the inconvenience of looking over a high fence to see the otters.

As soon as the pools were completed, Roy Grout, Manager of the Norfolk Wildlife Park, came over daily with Ronnie Mant and George Appleton to work on the enclosures. All through the dark winter days they struggled in a sea of mud, excavating trenches below the water table, driving in fencing stakes and putting up hundreds of metres of chain-link netting topped with an overhang of sheet steel. Gates were hung, thresholds concreted and electricity laid on to the fast growing line of enclosures.

The River Waveney bordering the Otter Trust at Earsham, near Bungay in Suffolk.

The first of the otter breeding enclosures under construction at the Otter Trust in the winter of 1975.

The farmhouse with its pamment floors and oak beams over four hundred years old, needed extensive alterations to equip it with central heating and septic tank drainage. Some rooms were enlarged by removing partition walls and Elizabethan fireplaces came to light in the living room and in the bedroom above. We were fascinated to find the interior walls were made of wattle and daub, basically hazel stakes tied together with coarse string, then plastered with a mixture of mud and cow dung. They were remarkably strong and the string was impossible to break with the bare hands despite its four centuries of life.

Thanks to the efficiency of our builders the house was ready for occupation by Christmas and only a few days earlier the first of the otters arrived to occupy some of the new enclosures.

Although we kept the Wildlife Park at Great Witchingham, we sold our cottage there some weeks before moving to River Farm. This meant that our two tame European otters, Kate and Lucy, who lived in the garden of the cottage, were temporarily homeless and the only accommodation available at the time consisted of a pair of large dog kennels with outside runs in each of which we put a steel bath. It was far from ideal, but adequate for two or three weeks. We made sure that the first two enclosures to be completed at River Farm were those close to the house where Kate and Lucy were to live and one Saturday I made the journey to collect them. It was with a sense of relief that I returned home with both otters safely in their boxes in the back of the car and summoned Jeanne to share the pleasure of watching them enjoy for the first time the space of the stream-fed pools in their new pens. Where the fence dividing the enclosures crossed the stream we had constructed stickles or barriers made of steel rods five centimetres apart in angle-iron frames driven

102

deep into the mud at the bottom of the stream. The top of each frame was clear of the water and fixed to the bottom of the fence. As the ends were embedded in each bank we felt sure the stickles were otter proof.

Lucy, always more highly-strung than her sister Kate, had shown signs of stress during her sojourn in the dog kennel and before we moved had held Jeanne's arm tightly in her forepaws as if begging not to be left behind. For this reason I decided to release her into her new home first. When I opened the box she walked out quietly, turned to look at both of us and then slipped into the pool. For ten minutes or so she dived and spun somersaulting and cork-screwing through the water in sheer joy. Then to our horror she disappeared and the water in her pool was stilled. My first thought was that she might have become wedged in the bars of the stickle, then Jeanne saw a movement in the stream outside the enclosure and there was Lucy happily playing.

At first we were not unduly worried for she was accustomed to going for walks with us and swimming at liberty in the river or in the sea and we rarely had any trouble in picking her up again when it was time to go home.

Realizing that she was in strange surroundings we both set off mainly to keep in contact and give her confidence. Lucy thought the whole affair was great fun and kept running back to Jeanne only to dart off again whenever we attempted to catch her. Once she left the stream and crossed the raised bank along the river walk to dive into the main river. This caused us some concern since we could no longer keep up with her if she decided to go exploring. Twenty minutes later she returned and joined us as we walked back towards the house, but as we approached the pens she doubled back into the stream again. Once she came back to me and stood up, her forepaws resting against my legs, but when I bent down to pick her up she wriggled free, slippery as an eel.

Lucy aged twelve weeks finds a piece of rotten wood to play with.

It was dusk and Lucy was beginning to show signs of tiring. She spent less time in the water, kept closer to us and when Jeanne sat on the ground she climbed onto her lap. I assumed that the game was safely over, but at that moment a low jet screamed over our heads and Lucy, terrified, fled back towards the river. We followed her in the gathering darkness and caught a glimpse of her as she ran down the bank into the main stream. She dived at once and disappeared.

At first we waited, expecting her to show up and when nothing happened we imagined she had gone off exploring again so we separated, Jeanne walking along the bank upstream, calling to her, while I did the same thing downstream. We kept it up for the next two hours, but of Lucy there was no sign. Later that night I took a torch and walked up and down the river calling her name for more than an hour but saw nothing. At dawn I went out again walking the river and calling but only the lapwings wailed in reply.

We were both certain that Lucy would not have remained away unless she was lost and during the following weeks we searched the river for miles upstream and down calling her name. We asked everyone locally to keep an eye open for her and our staff spent hours joining in the search. With no news our hopes began to fade.

A month later the water fell to summer level after an unusually dry spell. Along the river walk willow and alder boughs festooned with flotsam like old birds' nests were left high and dry by receding floods. Patches of mud appeared at the river's edge and I searched for signs of otter tracks. Suddenly I noticed the top of a wooden stake, encrusted with weed and barely showing; the current eddying round it had caught my attention and from the stake a piece of rope trailed downwards into the invisible depths. As I looked a cold shiver passed down my spine.

Climbing down the bank I stretched out over the water using a broken off bough to pull the rope towards me. It was covered by a layer of algae, grey-brown and slimy and as I began to haul it in I knew the thing was evil. When I had enough slack I climbed up the bank and went on hauling at the dead weight. A line of corks appeared hung with dripping weed, then some netting and finally the bamboo hoop of an old eel trap broke the surface. The net was roughly three metres long, cylindrical in shape with two chambers, each with a funnel entrance. It was half full of mud and debris but there was something else in the first chamber – the body of a drowned otter. It was Lucy.

We buried her that afternoon beneath the lawn close to the house and planted a lime tree over her grave.

She must have entered the net out of curiosity and being unable to find the way out again had drowned, probably while Jeanne stood on the bank above calling her. We both felt her loss, but it was worse for Jeanne as Lucy had always shown a special attachment for her and was very much her otter.

As soon as the house was finished the builders began the much bigger task of constructing the Trust's headquarters including public lavatories, entrance archway, shop, tea-room and a large exhibition hall (interpretative centre). Meanwhile the excavator had moved out onto the marshes to begin digging two lakes for waterfowl, each 0.5 hectare in size and two metres deep. Tens of thousands of loads of dripping peat were removed by a team of three dumpers

Lakes for waterfowl being excavated at the Otter Trust.

and transferred to the river's edge where a bulldozer reinforced the existing bank by piling the spoil three metres high along more than 400 metres of river.

The lakes took three months to excavate and two years passed before the soil dried out sufficiently for a bulldozer to level it off, grading it into the original bank. Since then it has been sown with grass seed and today it is indistinguishable from the rest of the embankment, which holds back the winter floods and protects the otter enclosures and our home from inundation should gale force winds coincide with exceptionally high tides. Then the whole valley from Beccles to Diss, more than 30 kilometres, becomes a shimmering expanse studded with isolated thorn bushes and clumps of willows and alders knee deep in the flood. Flocks of wintering Bewick's swans and rafts of mallard and wigeon rest secure far from the shore, while in the partially flooded fields at the sides of the valley, lapwing, golden plover and fieldfares spread out to feed at the water's edge.

From our house we can watch black wedges of wildfowl flighting up the valley against a dove grey sky and if we open the window at night we can hear the chuckle of passing mallard and the clear whistling whee-ohs of drake wigeon.

The author's house at Earsham seen from across one of the waterfowl lakes.

By midsummer the months of effort began to show through the chaos. Twenty-one large breeding enclosures for the otters had been completed and a raised walkway had been made in front of the first 12 of them.

The headquarters' buildings were well advanced, trees had been planted in the large car park and a fox-proof fence of heavy gauge galvanized weldmesh netting supported by pressure-creosoted wooden posts 2.5 metres high had been erected round the perimeter of the entire property. Waterfowl from Great Witchingham swam on the three lakes and otters lived in 13 of the 21 pens.

In all building operations it is the finishing touches which take the time and lead to a frustrating loss of impetus. By July we realized we were not going to be ready to open to the public at the end of the month as we had hoped. Minor yet vital things held us up like the tea-room and shop counters, which failed to materialize when promised, and the plumbing in the lavatories, which ran up against unforeseen snags. Only a concentrated final effort by everyone enabled us to open the Trust to visitors for the first time on 9 September 1976. But for the next 18 months work went on to complete the buildings and put the finishing touches to the Trust's grounds.

During that first summer, Lucy's sister Kate gave birth to two fine cubs, a dog and a bitch whom we christened Lucy. Gradually the new growth of grass and trees healed the scars made by the excavator, water plants of many species

106

flourished in the otter pools and the marsh quickly reclaimed the raw edges of the new lakes.

After six years of effort the Trust was firmly established. There were more births in the collection, membership topped the thousand mark and more than forty-four thousand people visited the Trust in its first full year. Meanwhile work began in earnest on more practical aspects of otter conservation, including population surveys, the creation of otter havens on the rivers of East Anglia and the installation of the first otter underpass beneath the coast road near Cley.

We hope to carry out the first reintroduction to the wild with young otters bred at Earsham within the next two or three years and as I finish this chapter the otter has been given legal protection in England and Wales, though not in Scotland. This was something for which we at the Trust and all our members had campaigned vigorously for three years.

There is still much to be done if the otter is to survive as a wild animal in Britain and the years ahead will be challenging and exciting. The Trust will, I am certain, grow in strength and influence so that through its work, future generations will still be able to watch and study the enchanting and elusive otter not only in Britain, but wherever otters live in the world.

Lucy's sister Kate gave birth to two cubs during 1976, the first European otters to be born at the Trust.

Bibliography

COCKS, A. H. (1881) Note on the breeding of the otter. *Proc. Zool. Soc. Lond.* 1881: 249–250.

ERLINGE, S. (1969) *Food habits, home range and territoriality of the Otter Lutra lutra L.* Zool. Inst. Lond.

FREEMAN, G. E. and SALVIN, F. H. (1859) *Falconry:* 350–352 London: Longman, Green, Longman and Roberts.

GREEN, J. (1977) *Otter Trust Annual Report*, Earsham: The Otter Trust.

GUDGER, E. W. (1927) Fishing with the otter. *Am. Nat.* 61: 193–225.

HARRIS, C. J. (1968) *Otters, A Study of the Recent Lutrinae.* London: Weidenfeld and Nicolson.

HEMMER (1920) Hell, Pavel Schutz und Erhaltung des Fischotters. *Natur und Mensch.* 2: April 1976.

MACDONALD, S. and MASON, C. F. (1976) The status of the otter (*Lutra lutra L.*) in Norfolk. *Biol. Conserv.* 9: 119–124.

MULLER, G. (1945) Series of five articles. *Yorkshire Post*, September.

NATURE CONSERVANCY COUNCIL (1977) *Nature Conservation and Agriculture*, London.

PARKER, J. (1977) Personal communication.

PIKE, O. G. (1950) *Wild animals in Britain*: 87–99. London: Macmillan & Co.

SCHEFFER, V. B. (1953) Otters diving to a depth of sixty feet. *J. Mammal.* 34: 255.

SETON, E. T. (1926) *Lives of game animals.* 2: 642–709. New York: Doubleday, Doran & Co.

STEPHENS, M. N. (1957) *The Otter Report.* London: UFAW.

THOMPSON, D'A. W. (1910) *Aristotle's Historia Animalium*: 594b30–595a4. Oxford: Oxford Univ. Press.

TULLOCH, B. (1976) *Otter Trust Annual Report.* Earsham: The Otter Trust.

VEEN, J. (1975) Het voorkomen en enige gedragsverschijnselen van de visotter, *Lutra lutra* (Linnaeus, 1758), in Noord-Holland. *Lutra*, 17: 21–37.

WAYRE, P. (1967) Breeding Canadian Otters (*Lutra c. canadensis*) at Norfolk Wildlife Park. *Int. Zoo Yb.*, 7: 128–130.

WAYRE, P. (1972) Breeding the Eurasian Otter (*Lutra lutra*) at Norfolk Wildlife Park. *Int. Zoo Yb.*, **12**: 116–117.

WAYRE, P. (1975) A report on the Common Otter (*Lutra l. nair*) (Cuvier) in Sri Lanka. *Otter Trust Annual Report*, Earsham: The Otter Trust.

WAYRE, P. (1976) The disappearing otter. *Water Space*, 12–17, London: Water Space Amenity Commission.

WAYRE, P. (1976) *The River People*. London: Collins and Harvill Press.

WAYRE, P. (1976) Attuale situazione della Lontra in Italia e proposte per la sua conservazione. *Contributi Scientifici Alla Conoscenza Del Parco Nationale D'Abruzzo*. Rome.

WEBB, J. B. (Undated) *Otter spraint analysis*. Reading: Mammal Soc.

WEIR, V. and BANNISTER, K. E. (1977) Additional notes on the food of the otter in the Blakeney area. *Trans. Norfolk and Nor. Nat. Hist. Soc.* **24**: 85–88.

WEST, R. B. (1975) The Suffolk otter survey. *Suffolk Nat. Hist.* **16**: 378–88.

Index